Banned Books

Banned Books

Informal Notes on Some
Books Banned for Various
Reasons at Various Times
and in Various Places

By Anne Lyon Haight

Third Edition

R. R. BOWKER COMPANY
New York & London   1970

Published by the R. R. Bowker Co. (A XEROX COMPANY)
1180 Avenue of the Americas, New York, N.Y. 10036

Copyright © 1955 by Anne Lyon Haight

Reprinted with additional material by permission of author.

International Standard Book Number: 0-8352-0204-6
Library of Congress Catalog Number: 54-11650

Printed and bound in the United States of America

Additional material: Copyright © 1970 Xerox Corporation

To My Husband,

SHERMAN POST HAIGHT

PREFACE

In its review of the 1955 edition of *Banned Books,* the "Anti-quarian Bookman" made some important criticisms. It complained that the bibliography was incomplete. It noted that there was no mention of the massive underground literature. It called attention to the omission of Cleland and Frank Harris.

This new edition does not attempt to remove the basis for the criticism. *Banned Books* makes no pretense to exhaustiveness. It is a chronological list of books, banned from 387 B.C. into the 1960's, compiled only with the idea of showing the trend of censorship throughout the years and the change in thought and taste. It is a handbook, a quick reference work which touches upon most of the famous episodes in our sorry censorship history. The definitive work, which might be dreamed of, would be too vast an undertaking for the small yield of important knowledge that it would make available. Not all that has ever happened is necessarily worth the effort of assembling it.

Most of the books fall under a ban of religion, politics or morality, making the offense one of heresy, treason or obscenity. Among them are books which have withstood the condemnation of their times to become the classics of today, as well as many other important works which have suffered trials and tribulations. Censorship seems to erupt at various times and in odd places, depending upon the social pressures at work. If political problems are uppermost in the public mind, then political works will feel the resentment of anxious people. At this particular time in America, morality is a major issue, and writings that seem to relate to social behavior in ways that offend the majority view are subjected to more or less severe attacks. However, with few exceptions, out and out pornographic books have been omitted here, as they are too obvious and too voluminous. It is felt they would also change the character of the book.

Censorship in the modern world has rather generally ceased to be a systematic social practice, particularly in the Western nations, and as time goes on fewer books have been tried in court. The situation was very well described in THE FREEDOM TO READ, a joint declaration of the American Library Association and the American Book Publishers Council, which reads in part: "The freedom to read is essential to our democracy. It is under attack. Private groups and public authorities in various parts of the country are working to remove books from sale, to censor textbooks, to label controversial books, to distribute lists of objectionable books or authors and to purge libraries. These actions apparently rise from a view that our national tradition of free expression is no longer valid; that censorship and suppression are needed to avoid the subversion of politics and the corruption of morals." Although examples of this unofficial censorship are shown here, we can not easily address ourselves to these small daily murders of words and ideas except to note that they exist and to hope that the reader does not forget them.

In updating *Banned Books,* it has been decided to leave the original text relatively intact, making only those changes necessitated by new information or new interests on the part of readers. It should be pointed out that reported instances of censorship are heavily biased toward events in the English-speaking world in the expectation that censorship is of most acute concern to the readers of this book, whose native language is English and whose interests are likely to be tied particularly to the United States. The bibliography has been revised; some titles have been dropped, others added. Many of the works cited have their own bibliographies, and any interested reader can go as far and in as many directions as he pleases in his study of censorship.

The author wishes to thank Mr. Morris L. Ernst for his many years of interest in and devotion to this work.

MAY 1970   ANNE LYON HAIGHT

CONTENTS

INDEX

Informal Notes

Informal Notes

ON BANNED BOOKS

HOMER. (c.850 B.C.)
The Odyssey.

387 B.C. Greece: Plato suggested expurgating Homer for immature readers.

A.D. 35. Rome: Caligula tried to suppress *The Odyssey* because it expressed Greek ideals of freedom—dangerous in autocratic Rome.

SOCRATES. (c.470–399 B.C.)

399 B.C. Socrates accused "firstly, of denying the gods recognized by the state and introducing new divinities, and, secondly of corrupting the young." Found guilty, he was condemned to death. Accounts of the events are in Xenephon's *Memorabilia* and Plato's *Apology*. Western history of censorship begins here. Although Socrates left no writings, his forthrightness as teacher and philosopher exposed him to the punishments of the state.

CONFUCIUS. (551–478 B.C.)
Analects. (Sayings of Confucius and His Disciples)

c.250 B.C. China: The first ruler of the dynasty of Ts'in wishing to abolish the feudal system, consigned to the flames all books relating to the teachings of Confucius; he also buried alive hundreds of his disciples.

221 B.C. The Emperor Chi Huang Ti disapproved of the traditional culture of China, considered it moribund, and persecuted the literati who were its apostles. He burned the *Analects* and all extant books except practical works on medicine, divinations and husbandry, but preserved those in the Imperial Library.

ARISTOPHANES. (c.448–c.380 B.C.)
Clouds, 423 B.C.
Lysistrata, c. 411 B.C.

423 B.C. Greece-Athens: *Clouds* was a play in which Socrates was pilloried as a typical representative of impious and destructive speculations.

66 A.D. His comedies were considered obscene by Plutarch.

1930 United States: Customs ban lifted on *Lysistrata.* During the period of prohibition the book was published and sold for as little as thirty-five cents; and the drama was played in New York and Philadelphia, as adapted by Gilbert Seldes.

1955 United States: In a successful challenge of the Comstock Act of 1873 which empowered the Postmaster General to rule on obscenity of literature sent through the mail, *Lysistrata* was declared mailable.

OVID, PUBLIUS. (43 B.C.–c. A.D. 17)
*Ars Amatoria, c.*1 B.C.
Elegies, B.C.

A.D. 8 Rome: The Emperor Augustus banished Ovid for writing *Ars Amatoria* and for an unknown act of folly. He was sent to the Greek town of Tomi, near the mouth of the Danube, where he died in exile eight years later.

1497 Rome: The works of Ovid were cast, with those of Dante and his friend Propertius, into the great bonfire of Savonarola, as erotic, impious, and tending to corrupt.

1599 England: *Certaine of Ovid's Elegies* (c.1595), translated by Christopher Marlowe, were burned in Stationer's Hall by order of the Archbishop of Canterbury, because of its immoral tendencies.

1928 United States: The Customs still barred *Ars Amatoria,* although inexpensive editions were sold freely within the barrier.

1929 San Francisco: *Ars Amatoria* banned.

APULEIUS, LUCIUS. (c. A.D. 125–)
De Asino Aureo. (The Golden Ass)

1931 United States: Import ban raised on this book which had been freely circulated since 1928.

THE BIBLE.

553 Italy-Rome: Emperor Justinian issued a decree commanding exclusive use of the Greek and Latin versions of the *Bible* and forbidding the *Midrash,* but accepting the Hebrew exposition of the *Old Testament.*

1409 England: The Synod of Canterbury at St. Paul's, London, issued a decree forbidding the translation of the Scripture from one tongue to another, and the reading of a translation later than that of John Wycliffe under penalty of greater excommunication, unless special license be obtained.

1525–26 The *New Testament,* partially translated by William Tyndale was printed at Cologne, as it was violently opposed by the clergy in England. He fled to Worms where he continued to publish clandestinely. The sheets of 6,000 copies of the *Testament* were smuggled into England where they were publicly burned by the dignitaries of the Church, thus becoming the first printed book to be banned in England.

1535 The *Old* and *New Testaments* translated by Miles Coverdale was the first complete *Bible* to be printed in English. Not being licensed by Church or State it had to be printed on the Continent.

1538 France-Paris: Regnault, famous printer of English books, was seized by the Inquisition and imprisoned while printing the "great" *Bible* for Cromwell, the sheets of which were destroyed.

1551 Spain: *The Inquisitorial Index of Valentia* (supplement) forbade *Bibles* in Spanish or any other vernacular.

1554 *The Inquisitorial Index of Valladolid* listed 103 editions of the *Bible* condemned because of errors and heresies to suppression, correction or cancellation.

1555 England: A proclamation by Queen Mary commanded "that no manner of persons presume to bring into this realm any mss., books, papers, etc. in the name of Martin Luther, John Calvin, Miles Coverdale, Erasmus, Tyndale, etc. or any like books containing false doctrines against the Catholic faith."

1560 Switzerland: The Geneva or *"Breeches Bible"* went into

140 editions between 1560 and 1644, although it was forbidden in the churches.

1611 England: Copyright in the King James Version rests perpetually in the Crown. Permission to reprint has been given to Oxford, Cambridge, Eyre & Spottiswoode and William Collins. Because of Crown copyright, no authorized Bible in English was printed in what is now the United States until after the Revolution.

1624 Germany: The *Bible* translated by Martin Luther in 1534 which had been the most widely read book in the country was condemned to the flames by Papal authority.

1631 England: In the edition of 1,000 copies of the *Bible* printed by R. Barker and assigns of Peter Bill the word "not" was omitted from the seventh commandment. The printers were heavily fined and the edition so vigorously suppressed that few copies have survived. It was named the *"Wicked Bible."*

1782 United States-Philadelphia: Robert Aitken printed what is generally considered the first Bible in English in the United States although there is now accepted evidence that a Bible was secretly printed in Boston about 1752.

1900 Italy-Rome: Pope Leo XIII decreed that translations of the *Bible* in the vernacular were permitted only if approved by the Holy See.

1926 Soviet Union: The *Index* of the *Soviet Inquisition* stated in their directions to libraries: "The section on religion must contain solely anti-religious books. Religiously dogmatic books such as the *Gospel*, the *Koran*, the *Talmud*, etc. must be left in the large libraries, but removed from the smaller ones." It is said that the *Bible* is refused admittance.

1952 United States: The *Revised Standard Version* was attacked by a Fundamentalist minister because of changes in terminology.

1953 North Carolina: A leaf of the same edition was burned in protest by a Baptist minister.

1956 Soviet Union: The *Bible* published after a lapse of thirty-eight years.

THE KORAN. (Seventh Century)

1542 Switzerland: Protestant authorities at Basel confiscated the entire edition published by Oporinus, who promptly appealed to the scholars. Exonerated by Luther, the edition was released.

1790 Spain: Ban lifted by the *Index.* Every version had been prohibited, especially the Twelfth Century Latin Translation by Peter of Cluny "cum refutationibus variorum."

1926 Soviet Union: Restricted to students of history.

1953 United States: Published in a paperbound edition.

THE TALMUD.

4th–6th cent.: Compiled between these dates and with the Old Testament became the Bible of the Jews.

1190 Egypt-Cairo: With his *Guide for the Perplexed,* Maimonides, the Jewish philosopher, aroused the Christians' resentment which culminated in the first official burning of Hebrew books by orders of Dominicans, Franciscans, and others.

1244 France-Paris: *Talmud* burned on charges of blasphemy and immorality. The book was persecuted in various places for another 100 years.

1264 Italy-Rome: Pope Clement IV appointed a committee of censors who expunged all passages that appeared derogatory to Christianity. (Talmudic references to ancient paganism were widely misrepresented as criticism of the Church.)

1490 Spain-Salamanca: In an auto-da-fé, thousands of Hebrew books including biblical texts were burned by order of the Inquisition.

1926 Soviet Union: Reported that the *Talmud* and other religiously dogmatic books were left in the large libraries, but removed from the small ones.

ABÉLARD, PIERRE. (1079–1142)
Introductio ad Theologiam, 1120.
Lettres d'Héloïse et Abélard.

1120 France-Soissons: A provincial synod charged Abélard with religious heresy, forced him to burn his *Introductio ad*

Theologiam, and imprisoned him in the convent of St. Médard.

1140 Italy-Rome: All works banned by the Council at Sens and ordered burned by Pope Innocent III. St. Bernard called Abélard "an infernal dragon and the precursor of the anti-Christ."

1559 & 1564 Rome. All writings placed on the *Index.*

1930 United States: Customs ban lifted on *Love Letters.*

BACON, ROGER. (c.1214–c.1292)
Opus Maius, 1268.
Opus Minus, 1268.
Opus Tertium, 1268.

1257 England: Bonaventura, General of the Franciscan order, suspicious of Bacon's supposed dealings in the black arts, interdicted his lectures at Oxford, and placed him under the superintendence of the order in Paris, where he remained for ten years under injunction not to write for publication.

1278 Italy-Rome: After the death of his protector, Clement IV, his books were condemned by Jerome de Ascoli, General of the Franciscans, afterwards Pope Nicholas IV, and Bacon was put into prison for fourteen years.

DANTE ALIGHIERI. (1265–1321)
De Monarchia, 1310–13.
La Divina Commedia, 1472.

1318 France-Lombardy: *De Monarchia* was publicly burned.

1497 Italy-Florence: Works burned by Savonarola in the "bonfire of the vanities."

1559 Rome: *De Monarchia* banned by Pope Paul IV and the *Index of Trent* for asserting that the authority of kings was derived from God and not from God's Vicar on earth, the Pope.

1581 Portugal-Lisbon: *La Divina Commedia* prohibited by Church authorities until all copies were delivered to the Inquisition for correction.

BOCCACCIO, GIOVANNI. (1313–1375)
Il Decamerone, 1353.

1497 Italy-Florence: Manuscripts and printed parts were thrown into Savonarola's "bonfire of the vanities."

1559 Rome: Prohibited by the *Index* of Pope Paul IV, unless expurgated. The revisers retained the episodes; but transformed the erring nuns into noble women, the lascivious monks into conjurors, the Abbess into a Countess (21st story), the Archangel Gabriel into the "King of the Fairies"; and the Pope authorized the edition.

c.1600 France: Censured by the Sorbonne and condemned by Parliament.

1922 United States: The Post Office authorities of Cincinnati seized an expurgated edition, and the district judge fined the bookseller $1,000.

1926 Banned by the Treasury Department.

1927 The Customs Department mutilated a copy printed by the Ashendene Press, and returned it to Maggs Bros., London, with the text missing. C. H. St. John Hornby wrote a protest to the London *Times.*

1931 Ban lifted by the Customs.

1932 Minnesota: Ban lifted.

1933 Australia: Cheap editions banned.

1934 United States-Detroit: Seized by the police as salacious.

1935 Boston: Still banned by the New England Watch and Ward Society.

1953 England: On list published in *Newsagent Bookseller Stationer* of nearly 700 titles named for destruction by local magistrates.

1954 Swindon: Copies ordered destroyed as "obscene" by magistrate's court, but an appeal court reversed the decision.
United States: On blacklist of the National Organization of Decent Literature.

WYCLIFFE, JOHN. (c.1320–1384)
De Civili Dominio, 1376.

1377 England: Pope Gregory XI issued five bulls on May 22, attacking Wycliffe's doctrines as expounded in his treatise on civil lordship (*De civili dominio*) which had been read to his students at Oxford in the previous year.

1409 Bohemia-Prague: Pope Alexander V's bull ordering the surrender of all of Wycliffe's books was carried out under the instructions of Archbishop Sbynko of Prague, who burned 200 volumes of Wycliffe's writings in the palace courtyard, and at the same time excommunicated Jan Hus (q.v.) who sympathized with the English theologian.

HUS, JAN. (c.1373–1415)
De Ecclesia, 1413.

1413–1415 Bohemia, Prague: Hus, whose criticism of the church and whose sympathy with the teachings of John Wycliffe had led him into deep trouble with church authorities, was summoned to Constance in Switzerland and then tried in nearby Gottlieben on the Rhine for teaching false doctrine. Refusing to recant his propositions, he was condemned and burned at the stake.

SCHEDEL, HARTMANN. (1410–1485)
Nuremberg Chronicle, 1493.

1493 Italy-Rome: This great illustrated history of the world includes (plate CLXIX), a picture of the female Pope Joan and her baby, here said to have succeeded as "John VIII" on the death of Leo IV who died in 855. She is here said to have been of English origin, though born in Mainz; to have disguised herself as a man and gone to Athens with a learned lover; and later in Rome to have become so famous for knowledge of the Scriptures that she was finally elected Pope by general consent. She seemed to justify this choice until, during a procession to the Lateran Basilica, she suddenly broke down, gave birth to a son and died ignominiously. The earliest known mention of her is by Stephen de Bourbon who died in 1261. In 1400 an image of her was included among the images of most of the Popes in Sienne Cathedral. In 1600, at the request of Pope Clement VI, her name was changed to Pope Zachary. In 1493 the legend was generally believed, but the earlier doubts became more general, and the picture and account of Joan were piously inked over or cut out of many copies of this and other books. There has been much controversy as to the truth of the legend, and it is now generally thought to be false.

SAVONAROLA, GIROLAMO. (1452–1498)
Writings.

1497 Italy-Florence: Savonarola transformed the pleasure-loving Florentines into ascetics; and celebrated the annual carnival by the famous burning of the vanities, including works by Ovid, Propertius, Dante and Boccaccio.

1498 He was forced by tortures on the rack to confess his heresy in demanding church reforms, and in denouncing papal corruptions. After the ceremonial of degradation, he was hung on a cross and burned with all his writings, sermons, essays and pamphlets.

ERASMUS, DESIDERIUS. (c.1466–1536)
Moriae Encomium, 1512.
Greek Testament, 1516.

1512 England: *Moriae Encomium* (Praise of Folly), in which kings, bishops, popes, and all manner of people, were impiously shown to be subject to folly, delighted the Pope, but was prohibited in the Universities of Paris, Louvain, Oxford and Cambridge. It was written in the house of Thomas More.

1516 Switzerland-Basel: Erasmus dedicated his most important work, the *Greek Testament,* to Pope Leo X who lauded him for "exceptional service to the study of sacred theology and to the maintenance of the true faith."
England: His powerful Catholic friends, including Cardinal Wolsey, Charles V, and Henry VIII, urged Erasmus to declare against Luther. He refused, but engaged in a sharp argument with the reformers, and continued to attack the abuses of the church, while remaining loyally within its folds. While Erasmus continued to look at the religious question in a sane, rational and objective way, the Lu-

therans and Calvinists calumniated him as a traitor to their cause, and Rome denounced him for heresy.

1524 France-Paris: The Sorbonne forbade the sale or perusal of *Colloquia.*

1550 Spain: The *Index* condemned *Opera Omnia.*

1555 Scotland: Mary, Queen of Scots, forbade the reading of Erasmus.

1557 Italy-Rome: *De Conscribendis Epistolis Opus* forced to be corrected to conform with the Inquisition. On page 181, Erasmus crossed out all but six words.

1559 The *Index* condemned *Opera Omnia* more harshly than the works of Luther or Calvin.

1576 Pope Gregory XIII authorized an anonymously expurgated edition, published anonymously.

1612 Spain: *Spanish Index* devoted fifty-nine folio pages in double columns to damning Erasmus.

1930 Italy-Rome: Erasmus was not specifically mentioned in the latest edition of the *Index.*

MACHIAVELLI, NICCOLÒ. (1469–1527)
Discorsi, 1503.
Il Principe, 1513.

1555 Italy-Rome: Although Machiavelli had been the ambassador and advisor of Popes and Cardinals in his day, Pope Paul IV placed his works in the severest category of the *Index,* and Clement VIII made a fresh prohibition of a Lausanne edition of his *Discorsi.*

1576 France: Selected maxims from *Il Principe* translated into French, were attacked by the Huguenot Gentillet for its political views. Cesare Borgia was supposed to have been the "Prince." The author contended that "if all rulers were good, you ought to keep your word, but since they are dishonest and do not keep faith with you, you, in return, need not keep faith with them."

1602 England: The Elizabethans derived from Gentillet their idea of and hostility for *Il Principe.*

1935 Italy: Machiavelli's dream came true. *Il Principe* demonstrated disjointed Italy's need for an all-powerful dictator supported by a national army. Mussolini paid Machiavelli tribute by encouraging the distribution of *Il Principe* in thousands of cheap copies.

LICENSING

1501 Rome: Pope Alexander VI issued a bull against unlicensed printing.

1535 France: Francis I issued an edict prohibiting under penalty of death the printing of books.

1585 England: The Star Chamber assumed the power to confine all printing to London, Oxford and Cambridge, to limit the number of printers, to prohibit all unlicensed publications and to enter houses in search of unlicensed presses or books.

1637 Prohibition of the importation into England of books deemed injurious to religion, the Church or the government.

1643 Licensing act passed by the Long Parliament, provoking John Milton's *Areopagitica* (q.v.).

1660 Reaffirmation of the edicts of 1637.

1679 Licensing act expired, to be renewed for an additional seven years in 1685.

1695 Licensing ended in England.

1765 Search for and seizure of authors for libel declared illegal.

1967 Press censorship against obscenity ended in Denmark.

Official censorship in varying degrees is still practiced in most nations of the Western world, although prior restraint has disappeared in the democratic countries, while still being widely practiced in the Communist nations and in Spain and Portugal.

VERGIL, POLYDORE. (c.1470–1555)
De Rerum Inventoribus, 1499.

1671 Italy-Rome: Although the author had been enthroned Bishop of Bath in 1504, this work was placed on the *Index* because of a passage which suggests that the Church's discovery of Purgatory stimulated a market for indulgences. The volume, treating of the origin of all things, ecclesiastical and lay, was so well liked that it was translated into French, German, English and Spanish.

1756 All editions appeared on the *Index,* except those following the text sanctioned by Pope Gregory XIII.

MICHELANGELO (Michelangelo Buonarroti).
(1475–1564)
The Last Judgement.

1933 United States: Plate forty is a copy of *The Last Judgement,* made by Venusti from the original fresco in the Sistine Chapel, before the addition of clothing to the nude figures by Daniele Volterra, by order of Pope Paul IV, and with the permission of Michelangelo. This book was ordered from Europe by the Weyhe Gallery and Book Shop. They received the following official letter from an assistant collector of customs who, apparently, had never heard of the great painter.

> Sirs:—There is being detained . . . 2 packages addressed to you, containing obscene photo books, 'Ceiling Sistine Chapel,' Filles-Michael Angelo, the importation of which is held to be prohibited under the provisions of the Tariff Act. The package will therefore be seized and disposed of in due course as provided by law. You may however avail yourself of the privilege of applying to the Secretary of the Treasury . . . for mitigation of the penalty of forfeiture with permission to export, or please execute the Assent to forfeiture below, returning same . . . Respectfully, H. C. Stuart, Asst. Collector.

After being ridiculed by the newspapers, the Treasury Department realized the ignorant mistake and relinquished the book.

LUTHER, MARTIN. **(1483–1546)**
Opera Omnia.
Address to the German Nobility, 1520.

1519 Germany-Wittenberg: Luther nailed ninety-five theses, discussing the true meaning of Indulgences, to the Castle Church door connected with the University. The Theological faculties of Louvain and Cologne ordered copies of them to be burned on grounds of heresy.

1521 France: The Theological faculties of the University of Paris ordered the *Theses* burned.

1521 Italy-Rome: A Papal Bull by Leo X excommunicated Luther, and forbade printing, selling, reading, or quoting, his *Opera Omnia,* thereby creating a passionate interest in them. He also ordered a formal burning of Luther's effigy and books.

In three months 4,000 copies of *Address to the German Nobility,* in which he stated the causes of social discontent, were sold.

In five days 5,000 copies of the vernacular edition of the *New Testament* were sold.

1521 Germany: Charles V, on his own authority, issued an edict against Luther, and ordered his books seized. At the same time he sent him a safe conduct to appear before the diet of Worms. The diet issued an edict against him, and threatened to exterminate his followers.

Strassburg: A contemporary comment was: "Lutheran books are for sale in the marketplace immediately beneath the edicts of the Emperor and the Pope who declared them to be prohibited."

1525 Luther became the virtual leader of the German nation. He invoked a censorship of the "pernicious doctrines" of Anabaptists, Calvin and Zwingli.

1532 Luther turned the tables and demanded the suppression of the translation of the *New Testament* by Einser, a Catholic Priest.

1930 Italy-Rome: The works of Luther omitted by the *Index.*

1953 Canada: The Quebec Censorship Board banned the motion picture *Martin Luther* on the ground that it would antagonize the people of the predominately Roman Catholic province.

AGRIPPA, HENRY CORNELIUS. (1486–1535)
De Incertitudine et Vanitate Scientiarum et Artium,
1530.
De Occulta Philosophia, 1531.

1509 France-Dôle: Charged with heresy for his lectures at the University, Agrippa was forced to take refuge with Maximilian in the Netherlands.

1531 Netherlands: *De Incertitudine,* a sarcastic attack on existing sciences and on the pretensions of learned men, was banned as heretical.
Belgium: The author was imprisoned at Brussels for satires written on the scholasticism of the professors.

1533 Italy-Rome: Charges of magic and conjury were brought against the author by the Inquisition for *De Occulta Philosophia,* Book 1.

TYNDALE, WILLIAM. (c.1492–1536)
The New Testament of Our Lord and Savior Jesus Christ, 1525–6.
Practyse of Prelates, 1530.

1525–6 England: The *New Testament,* partially translated by Tyndale, was printed at Cologne, as it was violently opposed by the clergy who damned it as "pernicious merchandise." He continued the work at Worms and the sheets of 6,000 copies were smuggled into England where they were publicly burned by the dignitaries of the church; consequently only one complete copy has survived which is in the library of the Baptist College at Bristol. Cardinal Wolsey ordered Tyndale to be seized at Worms, but he took refuge with Philip of Hesse at Marburg.

1530 Germany-Marburg: Church and State authorities banned *Practyse of Prelates,* a treatise condemning the Catholic clergy and the divorce of Henry VIII.

1536 Belgium-Vilvorde Castle: Tyndale was imprisoned, strangled and burned at the stake with his translations of the *Bible,* although about 50,000 copies in seven editions were in circulation.

1546 England: Tyndale's books were ordered delivered to the Archbishop to be burned, because he had called church functionaries "horse-leeches, maggots and caterpillers in a kingdom."

1555 His books fell under the ban of Queen Mary's proclamation, and were forbidden in the realm for containing false doctrines against the Catholic faith.

1939 The Royal Society of Literature made a reprint of Tyndale's

New Testament to celebrate the 400th anniversary of the man who made the first partial English translation.

RABELAIS, FRANÇOIS. (c.1494–1553)
Pantagruel, 1533.
Gargantua, 1535.

1533 France: The first two parts of *Pantagruel,* published without the knowledge of the author, were listed on the *Index* of the Sorbonne, and on the official black list of Parliament.

1535 Italy-Rome: A Papal Bull absolved Rabelais from ecclesiastical censure.

1546 France: The third book of *Pantagruel* was published under the author's name "avec privilège du Roi."

1552 Taking advantage of the King's absence from Paris, the divines of the Sorbonne censored the fourth book on publication.

1554 Cardinal de Chatillion persuaded Henry II to raise the ban on the works of Rabelais.

1564 Italy-Rome: The *Index* listed Rabelais as "Rebelisius" in its severe first class.

c.1900 France: An imaginative Frenchman, Robertet, refined the coarse language of these books in an adaptation for children. The story of Pantagruel, the giant, son of Gargantua, the giant, their feasts, their wars, and adventures, told with a satiric humor had the same appeal to the imagination as Swift's *Gulliver's Travels.*

1930 United States: The Customs Department lifted the ban on all editions with the exception of those with so-called obscene illustrations, specifically Frank C. Pape's drawings for an edition of the Motteux translation.

1938 South Africa-Johannesburg: All works banned.

1953 The 400th anniversary of the death of Rabelais was celebrated in the literary world.

CALVIN, JOHN. (1509–1564)
Civil and Canonical Law, 1542.

1542 France: *Civil and Canonical Law* forbidden by the Sorbonne.

1555 England: Queen Mary's proclamation required "that no manner of persons presume to bring into this realm any mss., books, papers, by John Calvin . . . containing false doctrine against the Catholic faith."

1559 & 1564 Italy-Rome: All works listed for heresy in the first class prohibition of the *Index*.

SERVETUS, MICHAEL (Villanovanus Michael).
(1511–1553)
Christianismi Restitutio, 1553.

1553 France: The author's theological tracts, recast as *Christianismi Restitutio,* were secretly printed at Vienne, in Dauphine, France, by Balthazar Arnoullet. Imprisoned by the Inquisition, he escaped, was recaptured and burned at the stake with his books.

PONCE DE LEON, LUIS. (1527–1591)

1571 Denounced to the Inquisition for translating the *Song of Solomon* and for criticizing the text of the *Vulgate Bible,* Leon was imprisoned for nearly five years at Valladolid.

MONTAIGNE, MICHEL de (1533–1592)
Les Essaies, 1580–88.

1595 France-Lyons: Certain sections of the unexpurgated edition were banned for being tolerant of an easy morality (fifth chapter of third book, etc.).

1676 Italy-Rome: Listed in the *Index*.

SCOT, REGINALD. (c.1538–1599)
A Discoverie of Witchcraft, 1584.

1584 England-London: The author held that the prosecution of those accused of witchcraft was contrary to the dictates of reason as well as of religion, and he placed the responsibility at the door of the Roman Church. All obtainable copies were burned on the accession of James I and are now rare.

1586 At that time a decree of the Star Chamber greatly tightened the censorship laws.

STUBBS, JOHN. (c.1543–1591)
The discoverie of a gaping gulf where into England is
likely to be swallowed by another French marriage,
1579.

1579 England-London: A virulent attack on the proposed marriage between Queen Elizabeth and the Duke of Anjou.
The author was condemned to have his right hand cut off
by means of a cleaver driven through the wrist by a mallet.
Stubbs thereupon raised his hat with his left hand and
cried, "God save the Queen."

The copies of the book were burned in the kitchen stove
of Stationer's Hall.

TASSO, TORQUATO. (1544–1595)
Gerusalemme Liberata, 1581–93.

1595 France: Suppressed by Parliament as containing ideas subversive to the authority of kings. *Gerusalemme Conquis-
tata,* written and published in 1592, was a revision exclud-
ing the suppressed material.

PARSONS, ROBERT. (1546–1610)
A Conference about the next Succession to the Crowne
of Ingland, 1594.

1603 England-London: The intention of the book was to support
the title of the Infanta against that of James I, after the
death of Queen Elizabeth. The authors were Parsons the
Jesuit, Cardinal Allen, and Sir Francis Englefield. The book
was rigorously suppressed by Parliament, which enacted that
"whosoever should be found to have it in their house should
be guilty of high treason." The printer is said to have been
hung, drawn and quartered.

1683 Oxford: Condemned by the university and burned in the
quadrangle particularly because of that which says "Birth-
right and proximity of blood do give no title to rule or government."

CERVANTES SAAVEDRA, MIGUEL de. (1547–1616)

The Life and Exploits of the Ingenious Gentleman Don Quixote De La Mancha, first part, 1605—second part 1615.

1624 Portugal-Lisbon: A few paragraphs were proscribed by the Spanish *Index.*

1640 Spain-Madrid: Placed on the *Index* for one sentence: "Works of charity negligently performed are of no worth."

RALEIGH, SIR WALTER. (1552–1618)

The History of the World, 1614.

1614 England: Suppressed by James I "for divers exceptions, but especially for being too saucy in censuring Princes."

THOMAS, WILLIAM. (d.1554)

The Historie of Italie, 1549.

1554 England-London: This book gave great offense to Queen Mary because of its criticism of the Italian clergy. The book was burned by the common hangman, and the author was hanged and quartered at Tyburn. A royal proclamation had been issued in 1538 by which no one was allowed to print any book unless he had received license from some member of the Privy Council or from a person appointed by the King, thus establishing the first regular censorship in England.

BACON, FRANCIS, BARON of VERULAM and VISCOUNT ST. ALBANS. (1561–1626)

Advancement of Learning, 1605.

1640 Spain: All works banned by the Inquisition and placed on Sotomayor's *Index.*

1668 Italy-Rome: Book IX of *Advancement of Learning,* dedicated to the King, was placed on the *Index, donec corrigetur* where it remained in 1948.

GALILEI, GALILEO. (1564–1642)
Dialogo sopra i due Massimi Sistemi del Mondo, 1632.

1616 Italy-Rome: Galileo was reprimanded by Pope Paul IV, and told not to "hold, teach or defend" the condemned doctrine of Copernicus, whose theory he had tried to reconcile with religion.

1633 *Dialogo* banned by Pope Urban VIII for heresy and breach of good faith. The author was examined by the Inquisition under threat of torture and sentenced to incarceration at the pleasure of the Tribunal. Galileo, although a white-haired old man of seventy, was compelled to kneel, clothed in sackcloth, and deny that which he knew to be true. He promised "that he would never again in words or writing spread this damnable heresy." He is said to have murmured as he rose from his knees: "Nevertheless it does move." By way of penance he was enjoined to recite once a week for three years the seven penitential psalms, although he felt "that Holy Writ was intended to teach men how to go to Heaven, not how the heavens go."

1642 On Galileo's death, his common-law wife submitted his manuscripts on telescopic and pendulum inventions to her confessor who subsequently destroyed them as heretical.

1954 United States: *Dialogo* translated into English for the first time since 1661; an event for scholars, as the book is extremely rare due to the almost total destruction of copies in the great fire of London in 1666.

HAYWARD, SIR JOHN. (c.1564–1627)
First Part of the Life and Raigne of King Henrie IV,
1599.

1600 England: At Whitsuntide, when fifteen hundred copies were ready for distribution, they were taken by the wardens of the Stationer's Company and delivered to the Bishop of London, in whose house they were burned. The book contained a dedication to Essex in terms of extravagant laudation and included a description of the deposition of Richard II. Essex's enemies at court easily excited the suspicion of the Queen that Hayward, under guise of an historical treatise, was criticizing her own policy and hinting at what might possibly befall her in the future.

SHAKESPEARE, WILLIAM. (1564–1616)
The Tragedie of King Richard the Second, 1597.
The Merchant of Venice, 1600.
King Lear, 1608.

1597 England: The original edition of *Richard the Second* contained a scene in which the King was deposed, and it so infuriated Queen Elizabeth that she ordered it eliminated from all copies. It was not reinserted until after her death, in the edition of 1608. Elizabeth complained that the play had been acted forty times in streets and houses "for the encouragement of disaffection."

1601 Sir Gilly Merrick paid players forty shillings to revive the play on the afternoon when the Earl of Essex sought to rouse London against the Queen.

1788 *King Lear* was prohibited on the English stage until 1820, probably out of respect to King George III's acknowledged insanity, when the royal duties were transferred to a Regent.

1815 Coleridge said: "Shakespeare's words are too indecent to be translated . . . His gentlefolk's talk is full of coarse allusions such as nowadays you could hear only in the meanest taverns."

1818 Thomas Bowdler, M.D., published the *Family Shakespeare* omitting "those words and expressions which cannot with propriety be read aloud in the family." "Bowdlerize" thereupon became synonymous with "expurgate."

1931 United States: *The Merchant of Venice* was eliminated from the high-school curricula of Buffalo and Manchester, New York. Jewish organizations believed that it fostered intolerance.

1953 Minority groups still felt that Shylock was depicted as an unfortunate characterization of a Jew and sought the suppression of the play.

LEIGHTON, ALEXANDER. (1568–1649)
An Appeal to the Parliament: or Sion's Plea Against the Prelacie, 1628.

1630 England-London: The book was a virulent attack on prelacy and an appeal to political Presbyterianism, to take the sword in hand. Condemned by the authorities, the author was seized and dragged to Newgate, where he was clapped in irons, and cast into a loathsome and ruinous doghole full of rats and mice. Tried by the Star Chamber Court, he was sentenced to a fine, to be degraded from holy orders, whipped at the Westminster pillory and have one ear cut off, his nose split, and to be branded with S.S. for "sower of sedition." This not being enough, he was returned to prison, whipped, lost his other ear and was imprisoned for life. The suppression of this book led to even stricter censorship laws by the Star Chamber.

JONSON, BEN. (1573–1637)
Eastward Ho, 1605.

1608 England-London: Jonson was imprisoned for collaborating with Marston and Chapman on the comedy, *Eastward Ho,* which was derogatory to the Scots. Released by the intervention of powerful friends, a feast was given in celebration, where Jonson's mother revealed that she had planned to give him poison if his prison sentence had been carried out.

MARSTON, JOHN. (c.1575–1634)
The Metamorphosis of Pigmalion's Image, 1598.

1598 England-London: The book is dedicated to the "World's mightie monarch good opinion," and the purpose of the author was to ridicule the immorality and evil tendency of a class of poems then fashionable, and to which Shakespeare's *Venus and Adonis* belonged. Characterizing the book as licentious, the prelates Whitgift and Bancroft ordered its suppression and destruction.

HOLINSHED, RAPHAEL. (d.c.1580)
Chronicles of England, Scotland and Ireland, 1577.

1587 England: Upon publication of the second edition, Queen Elizabeth's Privy Council ordered excised certain passages about the history of Ireland, which were offensive to her.

It was from this edition that Shakespeare drew material for *Macbeth, King Lear* and *Cymbeline.*

1723 Queen Elizabeth's excisions were published separately.

PYNCHON, WILLIAM. (1590–1662)
The Meritorious Price of our Redemption, 1650.

1650 Massachusetts Bay Colony-Boston: Pynchon's book was the first work to be publicly burned in what is now the United States. The treatise was at variance with Puritan orthodoxy on several points of theology. In view of the rigid adherence to the established doctrines enforced by the clergy, it was not surprising that Pynchon's opinions should have aroused a storm of wrath and indignation. His book was read with horror by the members of the General Court and condemned to be burned in the marketplace by the common executioner. Pynchon, a prominent citizen of the colony, was one of the original grantees of the charter. Though publicly censured, he escaped prosecution and left soon after for England.

DESCARTES, RENÉ. (1596–1650)
Les Meditations Métaphysiques, 1641.

1633 Holland: Descartes, a devoted Catholic, abandoned his treatise on Copernican beliefs when he learned that Galileo's treatise had been suppressed in Rome for supporting Copernicus's hypothesis of the earth revolving around the sun. Italy-Rome: Through the influence of the Jesuits, this author's works containing Copernican theories were placed on the *Index,* and forbidden in many institutions of learning until corrected or expurgated.

1665 Rome: *Meditations* was placed on the *Index* until corrected, as the whole system was opposed to the whole system of Aristotle.

1772 Rome: This edition was forbidden by the *Index* unconditionally, probably because it contained matter written by
others.

1926 Soviet Union: All philosophical works suppressed.

1948 Italy-Rome: *Meditations* and six other books still remained
on the *Index*.

PRYNNE, WILLIAM. (1600–1669)
Histrio-Mastix. The Players Scourge or Actors Tragae-die, 1633.

1633 England-London: This book, written with purity of conviction and moral earnestness, was brought to the attention of the King and Queen by Archbishop Laud. Prynne
violently denounced all theatrical plays, including those at
court, where they were frequently given, and he was therefore accused of a supposed attack on the Queen, who was
fond of the drama. She and her ladies had unfortunately
taken part in a performance of Walter Montagu's *Shep-
herd's Paradise*. In consequence the Star Chamber decreed that he be fined, imprisoned, branded and have his
ears cut off. His library was confiscated and his book was
burned by the common hangman.

Later, when Laud was on trial for alleged offenses, and
was sentenced to death, Prynne was one of the chief
prosecutors.

WILLIAMS, ROGER. (c.1603–1683)
The Bloudy Tenent of Persecution, 1644.

1635 British Dominions-Massachusetts Bay Colony: Denying
that the state had authority over conscience, and being out-
spoken in civil matters, Williams was "enlarged" out of
Massachusetts and went to Rhode Island, where he founded
Providence.

1644 England-London: *The Bloudy Tenent* was ordered by the
House of Commons to be publicly burned for the toleration of all sorts of religion. This book, written primarily as
an attack on John Cotton, contained a dialogue on intellectual freedom in civil and ecclesiastical governments and

an argument for democratic liberty and tolerance. Cotton
replied with *The Bloudy Tenent Washed and Made White
in the Bloud of our Lamb,* 1647. Williams retaliated in
1652 with *The Bloudy Tenent yet More Bloudy: by Mr.
Cotton's Endeavour to Wash it White in the Bloud of the
Lamb.*

1936 United States: The Massachusetts Legislature passed a bill
revoking the 300-year-old sentence of expulsion.

BROWNE, SIR THOMAS. (1605–1682)
Religio Medici, 1642.

1642 England: This famous work, written as a "private exercise
to myself," was printed without the knowledge of the author.

1645 Italy-Rome: The Latin translation was placed on the *Index*
by Pope Leo XIII, although Browne professed to be absolutely free from heretical opinions. He insisted upon his
right to be guided by his own reason when no specific
guidance was proffered by Church or Scripture.

MILTON, JOHN. (1608–1674)
*Areopagitica, A Speech for the Liberty of Unlicenc'd
Printing, to the Parliament of England,* 1644.
Eikonoklastes, 1649.
Pro Populo Anglicano Defensio, 1651.
Paradise Lost, 1667.
State Papers, 1676.

1476 England: Shortly after Caxton set up his press in Westminster, the crown forbade all printing except by Royal
permission. This pre-licensing continued for nearly 200
years, eventually calling forth the *Areopagitica.*

1644 This famed and eloquent plea for freedom of the pen was
delivered before Parliament and was published without
license in defiance of a restraining ordinance. *Areopagitica*
was condemned by Cromwell and the Parliament of Protestant England for such sentences as this: "And yet on the
other hand unlesse warinesse be us'd, as good almost kill a
man as kill a good Book . . . who destroyes a good Booke,
kills Reason itselfe, kills the Image of God as it were in the
eye."

1652 France: *Pro Populo Anglicano Defensio,* written as a reply to the attack on the commonwealth of Salmasius, was burned for political reasons.

1660 England: *Pro Populo Anglicano Defensio* was publicly burned. *Eikonoklastes* was burned by the common hangman at the time of the Restoration for attacking the hypocrisy of the religion of Charles I, and for arguing against the divine right of kings. The author escaped the scaffold only through the influence of friends.

1694 Italy-Rome: *State Papers,* published posthumously and surreptitiously, was listed on the *Index.*

1695 England: Pre-censorship of the press abolished and never again enforced.

1758 Italy-Rome: *Paradise Lost,* translated into Italian by Paolo Rolli, listed on the *Index.*

L'ESTRANGE, SIR ROGER. (1616–1704)
Considerations and Proposals In Order to the Regulation of the Press, 1663.

1663 England-London: This extravagant denunciation of the liberty of the press was dedicated to Charles II, and recommended a stringent enforcement and extension of the licensing act of May 1662. Master-printers, L'Estrange argued, should be reduced in number from sixty to twenty, and all workshops should be subjected to the strictest supervision. Severe penalties should be uniformly exacted, and working printers guilty of taking part in the publication of offensive works should on conviction wear some ignominious badge. He was rewarded for his vehemence by his appointment to the office of "surveyor of the imprimery," or printing presses, in succession to Sir John Birkenhead. L'Estrange was repeatedly imprisoned for his political views and writings and for his religious pamphlets. At times he was forced to flee the country for protection.

LA FONTAINE, JEAN de (1621–1695)
Contes et Nouvelles en Vers, 1665–71.

1675 France-Paris: Suppressed by the Lieutenant of Police for political satire.

1703 Italy-Rome: Placed on the *Index*.

1869 France: Publisher fined for producing the Fermiers-Généraux édition de luxe.

MOLIÈRE (Jean-Baptiste Poquelin). (1622–1673)
Le Tartuffe ou l'Imposteur, 1664–9.

1664 France: *Tartuffe,* a satire on religious hypocrisy, banned from the public stage by Louis XIV who, nevertheless, read it aloud to an audience which included high dignitaries of the church. The first three acts were given repeatedly at court, but Molière could not get permission for a public performance. During these years the church called him "a demon in human flesh," closed his theatre, and tore down his posters.

1667 While the King was away in Flanders, the play was given as *The Impostor.* The theatre was ordered closed by the Chief of Police, and the Archbishop of Paris laid a ban of excommunication on all who might act in the play, read, or see it.

1669 Permission was granted by the King to perform the play in public.

PASCAL, BLAISE. (1623–1662)
Lettres à un Provincial, 1656–1657.
Pensées, 1670.

1657 France: *Lettres* burned for being too free with the dignity of all secular authorities.

1660 Pascal having become converted to the Jansenist teaching, the *Lettres* aroused a storm of controversy because of their anti-Jesuit flavor. Louis XIV ordered that the book "be torn up and burned at the 'Croix du Tiroir' at the hands of the High Executioner, fulfillment of which is to be certified to his Majesty within the week; and that meanwhile all printers, booksellers, vendors and others, of whatever rank or station, are explicitly prohibited from printing, selling, and distributing, and even from having in their possession the said book . . . under pain of public (exemplary) punishment."

1789 Italy-Rome: *Pensées* placed on the *Index* "avec les notes de M. Voltaire."

LOCKE, JOHN. (1632–1704)
An Essay Concerning Human Understanding, 1690.

1683 England: Locke's theory of civil, religious, and philosophical liberty was too radical, and he escaped to Holland, the asylum of exiles such as Descartes, Erasmus, Grotius, and Spinoza, in search of liberty of thought. There he hid for some time under the name of Dr. Van der Linden. King Charles II deprived him of his studentship at Oxford, thereby closing the university to him.

1700 Italy-Rome: The French translation of *An Essay Concerning Human Understanding* was placed on the *Index.*

1701 England-London: The Latin version was prohibited at Oxford with the express ruling "that no tutors were to read with their students this essential investigation into the basis of knowledge."

RACINE, JEAN. (1639–1699)
Athalie, 1691.

c.1810 France: Under the imperial censorship of Napoleon, certain passages in *Athalie,* a religious tragedy alluding to tyranny, were canceled before a new edition was permitted.

FÉNELON, FRANÇOIS de SALIGNAC de la MOTHE. (1651–1715)
Explication des Maximes des Saints, 1697.
Les Avantures de Télémaque, Fils d'Ulysse. Imprime Par Ordre du Roi Pour L'Education de Monsieur le Dauphin, 1699.

1697 Italy-Rome: Although the author had been appointed Archbishop of Cambrai four years earlier, his *Explication des Maximes des Saints* was condemned by Pope Innocent XII as being against Christianity.

1699 France-Paris: Mme. de Maintenon caused the author's banishment, pretending to believe *Télémaque* a satire on herself and the King. Actually she was punishing him for opposing her marriage to Louis XIV.

DEFOE, DANIEL. (1660?–1731)
The Shortest Way With the Dissenters, 1702.
The Life and Strange Surprising Adventures of Robinson Crusoe, of York, Mariner, 1719.
Moll Flanders, 1721.
Roxana, 1724.
The Political History of the Devil, 1726.

1703 England-London: *The Shortest Way With the Dissenters,* a satire recommending that all dissenters be killed, was at first taken seriously by the Church. When the sarcastic import was discovered the book was burned and the author fined, imprisoned and pilloried.

1713 Defoe was prosecuted by the Whigs for writing treasonable anti-Jacobite pamphlets and imprisoned.

1720 Spain: *Robinson Crusoe* placed on the Spanish *Index.*

1743 Italy-Rome: *The Political History of the Devil* was listed on the *Index.*

1930 United States: Customs raised its ban on *Moll Flanders* and *Roxana.*

SWIFT, JONATHAN. (1667–1745)
A Tale of a Tub Written for the Universal Improvement of Mankind, 1704.
The Predictions for the Ensuing Year by Isaac Bickerstaff, 1708.
Drapier Letters, 1724.
Gulliver's Travels, 1726.

1708 Ireland: The *Predictions for the Ensuing Year* was burned as "such uncanny prescience could not otherwise than signify collusion with the evil one himself."

1724 *Drapier Letters.* Printed anonymously, the letters protested the introduction of a half-penny coin into Ireland on the ground that heavy profits from the coinage would accrue to favorites at the English Court. The Irish nation was so aroused that all efforts by Robert Walpole to prosecute the printer or to identify Swift as the author were frustrated.

1726 Privately printed and published anonymously, *Gulliver's Travels,* a satire on courts, political parties and statesmen, was denounced on all sides as wicked and obscene.

1734 Italy-Rome: *A Tale of a Tub,* charged with ridicule of papists and dissenters, was listed on the *Index.*

1841 Listed in the catalogue of Pope Gregory XVI.

1881 Ban lifted by Pope Leo XIII.

CURLL, EDMUND. (1675–1747)

1716 Curll, a publisher and bookseller, appeared before the bar of the House of Lords for publishing matter relating to members of the House. He was called again in 1721.

1727 Perpetually in trouble with the law, in this year Curll was found guilty of an obscene libel for publication of a scandalous book, *Venus in the Cloister.* This is the first recorded instance of a conviction on grounds of obscenity in the English-speaking world. A similar case in 1708 led to the dismissal of an indictment against a printer for publishing a bawdy book, because, as the Justice said, "there is no law against it."

SWEDENBORG, EMANUEL. (1688–1772)
Principia; or the First Principles of Natural Things,
1721.
Amor Conjugalis, 1768.

1738 Italy-Rome: *Principia* placed on the *Index* where it remained in the 1948 edition.

1909 United States-Philadelphia: *Amor Conjugalis* was seized by the Post Office authorities on grounds of obscenity.

1930 Soviet Union: All works banned.

MONTESQUIEU, BARON CHARLES LOUIS.
(1689–1755)
Lettres Persanes, 1721.
L'Esprit des Lois, 1748.

1721 France: *Lettres Persanes,* a satire on the social, political, ecclesiastical, and literary follies of the day, was published anonymously. It so shocked Fleury that Montesquieu was not admitted to the Academy until seven years after publication.

Italy-Rome: *Lettres Persanes* listed on the *Index,* where it remained in 1948.

1751 France: The Sorbonne planned but did not carry out a regular censure of the author for denouncing the abuse of the French monarchical system in *L'Esprit des Lois.*

Italy-Rome: Prohibited by the church authorities, although not with the entire approval of the Pope.

RICHARDSON, SAMUEL. (1689–1761)
Pamela; or Virtue Rewarded, 1740.

1755 Italy-Rome: The French translation by Abbé Prévost was listed on the *Index.*

England: This volume was abridged, not for moral reasons, but for length, and given as a reward of virtue to children who excelled in their lessons. Sir Walter Scott feared *Pamela* would rather "encourage a spirit of rash enterprise than vigorous resistance."

Charles Lamb pictured a young lad retreating from the book "hastily with a deep blush."

1948 Italy-Rome: Still listed on the *Index.*

VOLTAIRE (François Marie Arouet). (1694–1778)
Puero Regnante, 1717.
J'ai Vue, 1717.
Temple du Goût, 1733.
Lettres Philosophiques sur les Anglais, 1734.
Diatribe du Docteur Akakia, 1752.
Histoire des Croisades, 1754.
Cantiques des Cantiques, 1759.
Candide, 1759.
Dictionnaire Philosophique, 1764.

1716 France: The author was exiled to Tulle, and later to Sully, for composing lampoons against the Regent, the Duke of Orléans.

1717 The author thrown into the Bastille for writing *Puero Regnante,* and *J'ai Vue,* on grounds that they libeled Louis XIV.

1734 *Lettres Philosophiques sur les Anglais* condemned and burned by the high executioner on the grounds that it was "scandaleux, et contraire à la Religion."

Temple du Goût, a satire on contemporary French literature, was condemned. Copies were seized and burned, and a warrant was issued against the author, who was not to be found.

1752 Prussia: *Diatribe du Docteur Akakia,* a lampoon against Frederick the Great, caused the author to be arrested, and copies of the book to be burnt. In consequence, Voltaire ended his connection with the Court of Frederick.

Italy-Rome: *Lettres Philosophiques* placed on the *Index,* followed by *Histoire des Croisades* (1754) and *Cantiques des Cantiques* (1759).

1764 France and Switzerland-Geneva: *Dictionnaire Philosophique* banned.

1929 United States-Boston: *Candide* was seized on its way to a class in French literature at Harvard; but was admitted later in a new edition.

The Customs, after 170 years, discovered Voltaire and banned *Candide* as obscene, although it was being studied in college classrooms the world over as a literary masterpiece. The defense was prepared by two Harvard professors.

No one writer of the eighteenth century contributed so many books to the flames as Voltaire.

Erroneously attributed to Voltaire was one of the best known quotations on the freedom of speech: "I disapprove of what you say, but I shall defend to the death your right to say it." The phrase was coined by S. G. Tallentyre (Miss E. Beatrice Hall) in her book *The Friends of Voltaire,* London, 1906, and was not originated by Voltaire.

1935 Soviet Union: All philosophical works suppressed.

1944 United States-New York: Concord Books, Inc., issued a sale catalogue of 100 books for 49 cents each, including *Candide.* They were notified by the Post Office Department that the catalogue violated the section relating to the mailing of obscene literature, and that the title must be blocked out before it could be mailed. This was done.

1956 United States-New York: *Candide* made into a successful

Broadway musical, with text by Lillian Hellman, score by Leonard Bernstein, and directed by Tyrone Guthrie.

ARABIAN NIGHTS' ENTERTAINMENTS or THE THOUSAND AND ONE NIGHTS.
Origin unknown, first translation from the Arabic by A. Galland, Paris, 1704–12.

1927 United States-New York: The Customs held up 500 sets of the translation by the French scholar, Mardrus, which were imported from England.

1931 Ban lifted on the unexpurgated translation by Sir Richard Burton (1885–8), but the prohibition was maintained on the Mardrus edition.

FIELDING, HENRY. (1707–1754)
Pasquin, a Dramatick Satire, 1736.
Tom Jones, 1749.
Inquiry into the Causes of the Late Increase in Robberies, 1750

1730 England-London: Some of Fielding's early plays contained criticism of the political corruption of Sir Robert Walpole. The Prime Minister was so enraged that he forced a bill through Parliament which brought on the Licensing Act of 1737, enabling the Lord Chamberlain to license or suppress plays at will. Fielding turned to writing novels.

1749 France-Paris: *Tom Jones* banned on publication.

1750 *Inquiry into the Causes of the Late Increase in Robberies,* led to a parliamentary act governing the licensing of music halls in and near London.

1963 A somewhat frank film of *Tom Jones* was highly successful although widely criticized.

CLELAND, JOHN. (1709–1789)
Memoirs of a Woman of Pleasure, also known as *Fanny Hill,* 1749.

1749 England: Arraigned before the Privy Council for writing a literary obscenity, Cleland pleaded poverty. He was reprimanded and given a pension of £100 annually on condition that he not repeat the offense. The book went underground and remained the chief obscene classic for more than 200 years.

1821 United States: Banned in Massachusetts in the first known obscenity case in the United States.

1963 United States: Published openly by Grove Press, the book was attacked in the United States and declared obscene by the Massachusetts Supreme Judicial Court. The case was appealed to the United States Supreme Court, which reversed the decision and made the book permissible.

In other events during the period when the book was emerging into the open market, it was seized in Berlin, burned in Manchester, England, and burned in Japan.

ROUSSEAU, JEAN-JACQUES. (1712–1778)
Julie, ou la Nouvelle Héloïse, 1761.
Émile, ou de l'Éducation, 1762.
Du Contrat Social, 1762.
Lettres de la Montagne, 1763.
Lettre à Christophe de Beaumont, Archevêque de Paris, 1763.
Confessions, 1770.

1762 France: *Émile* condemned by the Parliament of Paris to be torn and burned at the foot of the great staircase; the Archbishop published a pastoral against the author, who went in exile to Geneva, his birthplace.

1763 Switzerland: Condemned by the Council of Geneva, whereupon Rousseau renounced his citizenship, attacked the Council, and the Geneva constitution, in *Lettres de la Montagne,* and fled to Neuchâtel, where he had the protection of Frederick the Great, who was the elected prince of this Swiss canton as well as King of Prussia.

Italy-Rome: Both books placed on the *Index.*

1766 Rome: *Du Contrat Social,* and *Lettre à Christophe de Beaumont, Archevêque de Paris,* were placed on the *Index.*

1806 *Julie, ou la Nouvelle Héloïse,* placed on the *Index.*

1929 United States: *Confessions* was banned by the Customs Department as being injurious to public morals.

1935 Soviet Union: All philosophical works forbidden.
1936 Works permitted in Soviet Union.

DIDEROT, DENIS. (1713–1784)
L'Encyclopédie, 1751–80.

1752 France: The first two volumes were suppressed by the King's Council for political and religious outspokenness.
1754 Louis XV issued a privilege for the continuation of the work.
1759 Although innocent of treason, this work was looked upon with suspicion and alarm in official circles. Consequently, the royal privilege was withdrawn. The work, however, was continued surreptitiously by the publisher, Le Breton, who had been censoring Diderdot's work without his knowledge. For a century and a half, scholars despaired of recovering Diderot's original text, for the manuscript had been destroyed as the matter was set in type, but a few years ago a volume containing Le Breton's corrections of the proof turned up and was acquired by an American collector.
   Italy-Rome: The first seven volumes were condemned by the *Index*.
1804 The complete work was placed on the *Index*.

STERNE, LAURENCE. (1713–1768)
A Sentimental Journey Through France and Italie by Mr. Yorick, 1768.

1819 Italy-Rome: The translation by Ugo Foscolo was listed on the *Index*.

HELY-HUTCHINSON, JOHN. (1724–1794)
The Commercial Restraints of Ireland Considered, 1779.

1779 England-London: Hely-Hutchinson, borrowing from Adam Smith, wrote what Lecky called "one of the best specimens of political literature in Ireland," which accused England of maintaining policies damaging to Irish trade. His work was condemned and is reported to be the last work burned by the common hangman.

KANT, IMMANUEL. (1724–1804)
Critique of Pure Reason, 1781.
Die Religion Innerhalb der Grenzen der Blossen Vernunft, 1793.

1793 Prussia: *Die Religion Innerhalb der Grenzen der Blossen Vernunft,* second part, was suppressed by the strong, Lutheran Prussian State because it was opposed to the literal doctrines of the Lutheran Church.

1793 Königsberg: Both parts were published, and Frederick William II promptly forbade the author to lecture or write on religion, not so much because of his religious unorthodoxy, as for his supposed sympathy with French revolutionary ideas.

1827 Italy-Rome: *Critique of Pure Reason,* in the Italian, was placed on the *Index.*

1928 Soviet Union: All works banned.

1939 Spain: Franco purged the libraries of "such disgraceful writers" as Kant.

CASANOVA de SEINGALT, GIOVANNI JACOPO. (1725–1798)
Mémoires: Écrites par lui-même, 1826–38.

1820 Germany-Leipzig: The original manuscript was confined to the safe of the publisher, Brockhaus, and never published in unexpurgated form until the twentieth century, although it was an invaluable record of morals, manners and etiquette of the eighteenth century.

1834 Italy-Rome: Placed on the *Index.*

1863 France: Condemned by "le grand procès de Lille."

1929 United States: An unexpurgated edition translated by Arthur Machen, with an appreciation by Havelock Ellis, was sold freely.

1931 Customs ban on imported copies was lifted, except for editions containing risqué illustrations.

1933 Ireland: Banned.

1934 United States-Detroit: Seized by the police.
1935 Italy: Banned by Mussolini.

GOLDSMITH, OLIVER. (1728–1774)
History of England, 1764.

1823 Italy-Rome: The Italian translation was listed on the *Index,* *"donec corrigetur."*

1948 *An abridged History of England from the Invasion of Julius Caesar to the Death of George II,* remained on the *Index.*

BEAUMARCHAIS, PIERRE AUGUSTIN CARON de. (1732–1799)
Le Barbier de Séville, 1773.
Mémoires, 1774.
Le Mariage de Figaro, 1778.

c.1770–c.1780 During his service as a secret agent of Louis XV and Louis XVI, Beaumarchais traveled abroad to seize writings condemning Mme. Du Barry and Marie Antoinette.

1773 For two years *Le Barbier de Séville* was forbidden to be performed on the stage. A revised version was successful in 1775.

1774 France: *Mémoires* was condemned to flames by Parliament for criticizing the state powers.

1778 *Le Mariage de Figaro* was suppressed for six years by Louis XVI at court and in public performances on the ground of profound immorality. The author was imprisoned in St. Lazare.

1792 Beaumarchais was charged with treason against the Republic and his works were suppressed. Released, he became an émigré for four years.

LORD CHAMBERLAIN.

1737 England: By the Licensing Act of this year the Lord Chamberlain was empowered to license plays, giving rise to the popular phrase "legitimate theater." The history of theatre censorship is itself long and complicated, and extends at least from medieval Europe down to the present. But the particular function of the Lord Chamberlain led to many clashes over works that have since become classics—even so seemingly harmless a piece as Gilbert and Sullivan's *Mikado*.

1968 The power of the Lord Chamberlain to license plays was revoked by Parliament.

FORSKÅL, PETER. (1736–1763)

1759 Sweden: After being rebuffed by the faculty of the University at Uppsala, and by the Chancery Council of Sweden, which possessed the final authority to license printing, Forskål privately printed his *Thoughts on Civil Liberty*. He was reprimanded by the King, and the Swedish Parliament established an investigating committee.

1766 As a result of the Forskål episode, censorship was abolished in Sweden.

GIBBON, EDWARD. (1737–1794)
The History of the Decline and Fall of the Roman Empire, 1776–88.

1783 Italy-Rome: The first volume, in Italian (1779), was placed on the *Index* because it contradicted much official church history. In his vindication, which refers to attacks, more by Protestants than by Catholics, Gibbon says: "I stand accused . . . for profanely depreciating the promised land . . . They seem to consider in the light of a reproach, the idea which I had given of Palestine, as a territory scarcely superior to Wales in extent and fertility; and they strangely convert a geographical observation into a theological error. When I recollect that the imputation of a similar error was employed by the implacable Calvin, to precipitate and to justify the execution of Servetus, I must applaud the felicity of the country, and of this age, which has disarmed, if it could not mollify, the fierceness of ecclesiastical criticism."

1826 England: An expurgated edition was published by Thomas Bowdler.

PAINE, THOMAS. (1737–1809)
The Rights of Man, 1791–92.
The Age of Reason, 1793.

1792 England: Paine's writings were the subject of bitter controversy in America, where he supported the cause of the colonies, and in England, where his attack on English institutions in his *Rights of Man* led to his indictment for treason and his flight to France.

France: Paine was imprisoned because of his hostility to the Jacobins.

England: Pitt commented: "Tom Paine is quite in the right . . . but if I were to encourage his opinion we should have a bloody revolution."

1797 England: T. Williams was prosecuted for publishing *The Age of Reason,* a defense of Deism against Christianity and Atheism, and was found guilty.

1819 Richard Carlile (*q.v.*), prosecuted for publishing the works of Paine, was heavily fined and imprisoned.

SADE, D. A. F., MARQUIS de. (1740–1814)
Justine, or the Misfortunes of Virtue, 1791.
Juliette, 1798.

1791 France: The authorities doggedly suppressed *Justine* and *Juliette,* and the Marquis spent much of his life in prison. Grandmothers, misled by the title, are said to have given *Justine* to their frivolous granddaughters to read as an object lesson.

1929 United States: *L'Oeuvre du Marquis de Sade,* from which the term "sadism" was derived, remained on the list of prohibited Customs importations, although pirated editions circulated surreptitiously within the barrier.

1948 Italy-Rome: Books still listed on the *Index.*

1955 France-Paris: A complete edition of the works of Sade in twenty-six volumes, begun in 1947, finally in 1954 came to the attention of the Commission Consultative, which, under a decree of 1940, was empowered to advise the Minister of Justice to initiate prosecutions. Despite such notable witnesses for the defense as Jean Cocteau, the publishers were fined and the books ordered destroyed, although most of them had long since been sold.

1962 England-London: *Justine* seized by British Customs.

1965 United States: Many of the suppressed works published openly.

CAGLIOSTRO ALESSANDRO (Giuseppe Balsamo).
(1743–1795)
Mémoires Authentiques de Cagliostro, 1786.

Maçonnerie Égyptienne, 1789.

1789 Italy-Rome: Cagliostro, alchemist and impostor, was imprisoned by the Inquisition for pamphlets advocating necromancy and astrology.

Spain: The *Mémoires* and *Maçonnerie Égyptienne* were placed on the Spanish *Index* for encouraging superstition.

1795 Italy-Rome: The author died in prison. He was arrested as a heretic on the denunciation of his wife and sentenced to death, but the punishment was commuted to imprisonment for life. His collection of books and instruments was publicly burned, including a manuscript which denounced the Inquisition as making the Christian religion godless and degrading.

JEFFERSON, THOMAS. **(1743–1826)**
A Summary View of the Rights of British America Set Forth in Some Resolutions Intended for the Inspection of the Present Delegates of the People of Virginia, now in Convention. By a Native, and Member of the House of Burgesses, 1774.

Mélanges Politiques et Philosophiques. Extraits des Mémoires et de la Correspondance de T. Jefferson.

1774 England: The pamphlet on the *Rights of British America* by the author of the Declaration of Independence was printed by sympathetic friends, without Jefferson's knowledge, and says "Our emigration to this country gave England no more rights over us than the emigration of the

Danes and the Saxons gave to the present authorities of their mother country over England." It contained material rejected by the Virginia Constitutional Convention. The Declaration of Independence is practically a transcript of this book. Popular in America, the British edition caused the proscription of Jefferson's name by the English House of Parliament.

1833 Russia: *Mélanges Politiques et Philosophiques* was banned for political reasons under Nicholas I.

GOETHE, JOHANN WOLFGANG von. (1749–1832)
Sorrows of Werther, 1774.
Faust, 1790.

1776 Denmark: *Sorrows of Werther* was prohibited under a strict censorship exercised by the Lutheran authorities.

1808 Germany-Berlin: The State authorities suppressed the production of *Faust,* until certain "dangerous passages" concerning freedom were deleted.

1939 Spain: Franco purged the libraries of the works of "such disgraceful writers" as Goethe.

RADISHCHEV, ALEXANDER. (1749–1802)
Putishestvie (Journey from Petersburg to Moscow), 1790.

1790 Russia: *Putishestvie,* a book of travel with emphasis on the evils of serfdom and Tsarist absolutism, was one of the most famous books suppressed by the Tsars. Catherine II declared that the book was an attempt to propagate the ideas of the French revolution, and ordered the edition burned by the public executioner. The author was sentenced to death, but the sentence was commuted to ten years in Siberia.

1801 Author granted amnesty by Alexander I, but, unwilling to "reform," he took poison the following year.

1935 Moscow: A facsimile copy of the first edition was published.

BARLOW, JOEL. (1754–1812)
Advice to the Privileged Orders, 1791–95.

1792 England-London: Eulogized by Fox on the floor of the House of Commons, whereupon the Pitt Ministry suppressed the work and proscribed the author.

SCHILLER, JOHAN CHRISTOPH FRIEDRICH von.
(1759–1805)
Die Räuber: ein Schauspiel, 1781.

1782 Germany: The Duke of Württemberg, annoyed with Schiller for running away from his medical post at Stuttgart to see his drama performed at Mannheim, put him under a fortnight's arrest and forbade him to write any more "comedies" or to hold intercourse with anyone outside Württemberg. The Duke was also irritated by a complaint from Switzerland of an uncomplimentary reference to Graubünden in *Die Räuber*. All the author's poetic dramas and philosophical works were written after this affair.

BABEUF, FRANÇOIS NOEL (Gracchus Babeuf).
(1760–1797)
Le Tribun du Peuple, 1794.

1794 France-Paris: Father of revolutionary socialism, Babeuf attacked, in his *Journal de la Liberté de la Presse,* later called, *Le Tribun du Peuple,* not only the fallen terrorists after the execution of Robespierre, but also the economic theories of the Directoire.

1795 Number 33 of the *Tribun* was burned in the Théâtre des Bergères, by the *jeunesse dorée,* foes of Jacobinism, as a cure for the economic disaster that followed the collapse of the vicious dole system.

1796 Number 40 of the *Tribun* rallied thousands of workmen under Babeuf's slogan, "Nature has given to every man the right to the enjoyment of an equal share in all property."

1797 The author was arrested, tried, and convicted, in spite of the efforts of his Jacobin friends to save him. He stabbed himself before being summoned to the guillotine.

CHÉNIER, ANDRÉ MARIE de. (1762–1794)
Avis au Peuple Français, 1790.
Ode à Charlotte Corday, 1792.
Iambes, 1795.
Jeune Captive, 1795.

1792 France: His political writings, including *Avis au Peuple Français* and *Ode à Charlotte Corday,* were privately printed and publicly banned.

1794 Paris: While imprisoned in the Saint Lazare by the Committee of Public Safety for protesting too violently against the Reign of Terror, Chénier wrote *Iambes,* attacking the Convention (the revolutionary legislature), and *Jeune Captive,* a poem of despair. He was guillotined, on a false charge of conspiracy, three days before Robespierre. The books were published the year after his death.

STAËL-HOLSTEIN, ANNE LOUISE GERMAINE de. (1766–1817)
Corinne, ou l'Italie, 1807.
De l'Allemagne, 1810.

1807 Italy-Rome: *Corinne* was listed on the *Index* for immorality.

1810 France-Paris: *De l'Allemagne,* extolling the merits of German culture, was condemned by Napoleon as "not French" in its political philosophy. The author was exiled from the country and her book was destroyed. She took refuge on her father's estate on Lake Geneva until the fall of the Emperor. The condemnation was no doubt due to Napoleon's personal animosity for Mme. Staël, and his fear of her ambitions, as her salon was largely devoted to organizing political intrigues against him. Her political views were alleged to be so contaminating that Mme. Récamier was exiled for frequenting her salon, since she was undoubtedly implicated as well.

STENDHAL (Marie Henri Beyle). (1783–1842)
Le Rouge et le Noir, 1831.

1850 Russia: *Rouge et Noir,* and all other works, banned by Nicholas I.

1939 Spain: Works purged by Franco.

1948 Italy-Rome: Still listed on the *Index.*

SHELLEY, PERCY BYSSHE. (1792–1822)
The Necessity of Atheism, 1811.
Queen Mab, a Philosophical Poem, 1813.
Alastor, 1816.
The Revolt of Islam, 1817.
Prometheus Unbound, 1818.
The Cenci, 1819.

1811 England: Shelley and his friend Hogg were dismissed from Oxford as mutineers against academic authority, for publishing *The Necessity of Atheism.*

1816 *Alastor* was rejected by a library on grounds of immorality.

1841 Moxon, the publisher, was convicted for publishing Shelley's works, which included such celebrated pieces as *Queen Mab, The Revolt of Islam, The Cenci, Alastor* and *Prometheus Unbound.*

1842 *Queen Mab,* privately printed because of its opinions on moral and religious matters, was prosecuted for blasphemy. The publisher was released upon giving up all copies in his possession.

GOODRICH, Rev. SAMUEL G. (1793–1860)
Peter Parley's Annual. A Christmas and New Year's Present for Young People, 1832.

1843 Russia: Prohibited unconditionally by Nicholas I. Goodrich, an American under the pseudonym of Peter Parley, wrote about 170 moral and historical tales for children. Seven million volumes were said to have been sold. They proved so popular that various pirated editions were published in England, illustrated by some of the famous illustrators of the day, including Cruikshank, Leech and Phiz.

HEINE, HEINRICH. (1797–1856)
Reisebilder, 1826–31.
Die Lorelei, 1827.
De la France, 1835.
De l'Allemagne, 1836.
Neue Gedichte, 1844.

1833 Germany: The Federal Diet issued a decree banning all works by members of a radical literary group called "Young Germany." Anticipating such suppression, and attracted by the revolution of 1830, Heine had taken up residence in Paris in 1831, where he wrote freely and received an annual stipend from a fund for political refugees.

1836 Italy-Rome: *De la France, Reisebilder* and *De l'Allemagne,* were placed on the *Index,* where they remained in 1948.

1844 *Neue Gedichte* was listed on the *Index,* where it remained in the edition of 1948.

1933 Germany: Works burned in the Nazi bonfires. (Heine, although born a Jew, embraced Christianity in 1825.)

1939 *Die Lorelei* listed as the work of Anonymous instead of Heine, for although his works were banned, the poem was too well loved to suppress.

1954 East Berlin: Works banned by the Soviet occupation authorities. Later republished.

BALZAC, HONORÉ de. (1799–1850)
LES Contes Drôlatique (Droll Stories) (1832–37).

1841 Italy-Rome: All works listed on the *Index.*

1850 Russia: All works banned.

1914 Canada: *Droll Stories* banned by the Customs and is still forbidden.

1930 United States: Customs ban lifted.

1944 New York: Concord Books, Inc. issued a sale catalogue of 100 books for 49 cents each, including *Droll Stories.* They were notified by the Post Office Department that the catalogue violated the section relating to the mailing of obscene literature, and that the title must be blocked out. This was done.

1953 Spain: Franco purged the libraries of "such disgraceful writers" as Balzac.

Soviet Union: Works published in large editions.

CIRCULATING LIBRARIES

19th century England: The high price of books led to the growth of circulating libraries which, for a modest subscription price, supplied to readers a continuous flow of popular novels. The most famous of these organizations, Mudie's, while never a monopoly, came very close to being one, with the result that the decision by Mudie's to buy or reject a novel often determined the fate of a book. The pressure thereby placed upon publishers to conform to the standards imposed by Mudie's made virtually impossible the honest treatment of thematic material by authors. The clashes of authors with their publishers are too numerous to mention, but the famous works that were excluded from the circulating libraries comprise a list of classic English fiction. George Gissing's *New Grub Street* is a vivid fictional account of an author unable to find a market for his works because of the tyranny of the system. George Moore's *Esther Waters,* Thomas Hardy's *Jude the Obscure,* H. G. Wells' *Ann Veronica* and Compton MacKenzie's *Sinister Street* were only four of the titles around the turn of the twentieth century which were excluded from circulating libraries.

The effect of this kind of "respectable" censorship on British literature is impossible to calculate, but it is against this background that some of the rebellious English authors of the period after World War I can be seen in a new dimension, e.g. Lawrence, Huxley, Graves.

OWEN, ROBERT DALE. (1801–1877)
Moral Physiology, 1836.

1877 England-London: Edward Truelove, a seventy-year-old bookseller and disciple of Owen, who had achieved great fame in the United States, was imprisoned for four months for selling *Moral Physiology,* which was considered designed to deprave public morals.

HUGO, VICTOR MARIE. (1802–1885)
Hernani, 1830.
Marion Delorme, 1831.
Notre Dame de Paris, 1831.
Le Roi s'Amuse, 1832.
Napoleon le Petit, 1851.
Les Misérables, 1862.

1829 France: Performance of the play, *Marion Delorme*, was prohibited by the official censors because it showed Louis XIII as a "weak, superstitious and cruel prince," and this depiction might provoke public malevolence and lead to disparagement of Charles X. Hugo appealed to the King. A royal veto sustained the prohibition; but Charles offered to raise the poet's pension from two to six thousand francs. After Charles was removed by the Revolution of 1830, the play was produced at the Théâtre Français and published for the first time, in 1831.

1830 Paris: The Inspector General of Theatres ordered the correction of such passages in *Hernani* as, "Thinkest thou that kings to me have aught of sacredness?" A literary war ensued: classicists and romanticists fought nightly in the theatre and out. The classicists hired professional claques. Théophile Gautier organized a troop of volunteers "resolved to take their stand upon the rugged mount of Romanticism, and to valiantly defend its passes against the assault of the Classics." In the end Romanticism triumphed; but not without a martyr, for a young man died fighting a duel over the play.

1832 *Le Roi s'Amuse* was prohibited after the first performance, by order of the Prime Minister, Guizot, for derogatory allusions to Louis-Phillipe. It was produced fifty years later under the supervision of the author.

1834 Italy-Rome: *Notre Dame* placed on the *Index*.

1850 Russia: All works banned by Nicholas I.

1853 France: Copies of *Napoleon le Petit* were seized by the police. This satire was written one year after the author had been banished by Napoleon III and began his twenty-year exile for criticizing the government.

1864 Italy-Rome: *Les Misérables,* published two years earlier, was listed on the *Index.* Removed from the *Index* in 1959.

HAWTHORNE, NATHANIEL. (1804–1864)
The Scarlet Letter, a Romance, 1850.

1852 Russia: Banned by Nicholas I in the "censorship terror." United States: Rev. A. C. Coxe argued "against any toleration to a popular and gifted writer when he perpetrates bad morals—let this brokerage of lust be put down at the very beginning."

1856 Russia: Ban lifted by Alexander II.

1925 United States: The screen version was made to comply with the demand of the Board of Censorship for the marriage of Hester.

ANDERSEN, HANS CHRISTIAN. (1805–1875)
Wonder Stories, 1835.

1835 Russia: Banned by Nicholas I during the "censorship terror." Ban removed in 1849.

1954 United States-Illinois: Stamped "For Adult Readers" to make it "impossible for children to obtain smut."

BROWNING, ELIZABETH BARRETT. (1806–1861)
Aurora Leigh, 1857.
Lord Walter's Wife, 1857.

1857 United States-Boston: *Aurora Leigh* was condemned as "the hysterical indecencies of an erotic mind."
England: Thackeray declined to publish *Lord Walter's Wife* because of its "immoral situation"; and it was excluded from the monopolistic circulating libraries (*q.v.*).

MILL, JOHN STUART. (1806–1873)
System of Logic, 1843.
Principles of Political Economy with some of their Applications to Social Philosophy, 1848.

1856 Italy-Rome: The *Index* listed these works, which epitomized the social and philosophical theories of the more educated English radicals of the day.

DAUMIER, HONORÉ. (1808–1879)
La Caricature, 1832.

1832 France: As a staff artist for the journal, *La Caricature,* Daumier did a satirical drawing of the King as Gargantua, for which he served six months in prison at Ste. Pélagie, and the journal was suppressed.

DARWIN, CHARLES ROBERT. (1809–1882)
On the Origin of Species, 1859.

1859 England-Cambridge: The entire edition of 1,250 copies was sold on publication date. The Master of Trinity College refused to allow a copy of the book to be placed in the Library, although Darwin was a graduate of Cambridge.

1925 United States-Dayton, Tennessee: John T. Scopes was found guilty of having taught evolution based on *The Origin of Species* in the high school, and was fined $100 and costs. Chief counsel for the prosecution was William Jennings Bryan, and Chief defense counsel was Clarence Darrow. As a result of the decision a law was passed forbidding any teacher in the State "to teach any theory that denies the story of the Divine creation of man as taught in the Bible, and to teach instead that man has descended from a lower order of animals." This law remained on the statute books until 1967.

1935 Yugoslavia: Prohibited.

1937 Greece: Banned under the Metaxas regime.

BLANC, JEAN JOSEPH CHARLES LOUIS. (1811–1882)
Organisation du Travail, 1840.

1839 France-Paris: The author tried to put into practice the principles of his work (abolition of competition, equalization of wages, immersion of personal interest in the common good) by establishing cooperatives financed by the state. The state initiated "National Workshops," a parody of Blanc's principles, involving a flat wage of two francs a day for cleaning the Gare Montparnasse, replanting trees on the boulevards, and digging up the Champ de Mars. Thousands of unemployed flocked to Paris. Blanc was held responsible for the disastrous consequences, and barely escaped to London. After he had left he was condemned to deportation, and his work suppressed until the fall of the Empire in 1870.

1840 Russia: All works banned by Nicholas I under the "censorship terror."

GAUTIER, THÉOPHILE. (1811–1872)
Mademoiselle de Maupin, 1835.
Mémoire de Charles Baudelaire, 1871.

1831–1853 Russia: *Mademoiselle de Maupin* was banned by Nicholas I during the period of "censorship terror."

1860 France: Gautier lost the wreath of the Academy for his writings.

1871 England: Robert Buchanan, always ready to criticize, denounced the *Mémoire de Charles Baudelaire* as "skillfully and secretly poisoning the mind of the unsuspicious reader."

1917 United States: The New York Society for the Suppression of Vice noticed a copy of *Mademoiselle de Maupin* in the window of McDermitt Wilson, booksellers. As it was opened at a "corrupting" illustration, the booksellers were tried in court and acquitted. The bookshop sued the Society for damages, won the decision after it had been once reversed, and was awarded $2500, plus accrued interest.

STOWE, HARRIET BEECHER. (1811–1896)
Uncle Tom's Cabin, or Life Among the Lowly, 1852.

1852 Russia: Banned under the "censorship terror" of Nicholas I.

1855 Italy-Papal States: The sale of the volume was prohibited, though not listed on the *Index.*

1858 Russia: Ban lifted on the Russian translation.

1955 United States-Bridgeport, Conn.: A dramatized version was protested by Negroes as putting them in an unfavorable light. For many years previous, "Uncle Tom" had been increasingly used as a derogatory epithet.

MARX, KARL. (1818–1883)
Rheinische Zeitung, 1842.
Manifesto of the Communist Party, 1847.
Das Kapital, 1867–95.

1843 Germany-Cologne: *Rheinische Zeitung,* a journal of advanced political and social ideas, was suppressed one year after Marx became editor. He was exiled in Paris and Brussels, but returned at the outbreak of revolution in 1848.

c.1845 France: Marx was expelled at the instance of the Prussian Foreign Office for contributing to the radical magazine *Vorwärts,* which was then liquidated.

1849 Prussia: *Neue Rheinische Zeitung* published "an organ of democracy," which advocated nonpayment of taxes, and armed resistance against Emperor Frederick William. Publication of the *Zeitung* was suspended, and the editor, Marx, was tried for treason. Although unanimously acquitted by a middle-class jury, he was expelled from the country. Being unwelcome in Paris, he made London his home for the rest of his life.

1878 Germany: Following two attempts on the life of William I, Bismarck persuaded the Reichstag to enact stringent measures against the Social Democrats, and prohibited their literature, including the *Manifesto.*

1929 China: The Nationalist Government sent armies against the sporadic Communist outbreaks in the provinces, and stopped, where possible, the reading of the *Manifesto* and *Kapital.*

1950–1953 United States: Marx's works, along with Communist writings generally, were heavily criticized in the United States. The Boston Public Library, under attack by the Boston *Post* for including Communist works in its collections, put the issue to a vote of its Trustees, who upheld the inclusion of such works by a 3–2 vote.

ELIOT, GEORGE (Mary Ann Evans). (1819–1880)
Adam Bede, 1859.

1859 England: *Adam Bede,* although a popular success, was attacked as "the vile outpourings of a lewd woman's mind,"

and was soon withdrawn from the circulating libraries of
the period.

WHITMAN, WALT. (1819–1892)
Leaves of Grass, 1855.

1855 United States: The poems shocked American puritanism
and English victorianism, although Ralph Waldo Emerson
wrote to the New York *Times,* calling the book "the most
extraordinary piece of wit and wisdom that America has
yet contributed."

The Library Company of Philadelphia was the only
American library known to have bought a copy on publication.

1868 England-London: After reading *Leaves of Grass,* Mrs.
Anne Gilcrist defended his use of banned words in *A
Woman's Estimate of Walt Whitman* and said: "A quarrel
with words is more or less a quarrel with meanings . . . If
the thing a word stands for exists (and what does not so
exist?), the word need never be ashamed of itself; the
shorter and more direct the better. It is a gain to make
friends with it, and see it in good company."

1881 United States-Boston: The District Attorney, at the urging
of agents of the Society for the Suppression of Vice,
threatened criminal prosecution unless the volume was expurgated. The book was withdrawn in Boston but published
in 1882 in Philadelphia.

Whittier, in a rage of indignation, threw his first edition
into the fire, although he himself had suffered persecution
for his abolitionist poems.

Wendell Phillips' comment was: "Here be all sorts of
leaves except fig leaves."

BAUDELAIRE, CHARLES PIERRE. (1821–1867)
Les Fleurs du Mal, 1857.
Les Épaves, 1866.

1857 France-Paris: The author, publisher, and printer were
prosecuted under the second Empire, for an "outrage aux

bonnes moeurs." Baudelaire was arrested and fined 300 francs.

1866 Belgium-Brussels: Six poems suppressed from *Les Fleurs du Mal* were published under the title of *Les Épaves,* and were widely circulated in France.

1949 France: Ban lifted.

FLAUBERT, GUSTAVE. (1821–1880)
Madame Bovary, Moeurs de Province, 1856.
Salammbô, 1862.
The Temptation of St. Anthony, 1874.
November (Written 1842).

1857 France-Paris: The author was taken to court for "outrage aux bonnes moeurs," as depicted in *Madame Bovary.* He was acquitted on the ground that the passages cited by the prosecution, though reprehensible, were few in number compared with the extent of the whole work. His counsel pleaded that in depicting vice, the author was only endeavoring to promote virtue.

1864 Italy-Rome: *Madame Bovary* and *Salammbô* were placed on the *Index.*

1927 United States: *The Temptation of St. Anthony* was unsuccessfully attacked by the New York Society for the Suppression of Vice.

1934 New York: *November* was seized at customs as obscene but released by literary experts of the Customs Bureau.

1935 New York: The Society for the Suppression of Vice attacked *November,* but Magistrate Jonah J. Goldstein discharged the complaint, saying: "The criterion of decency is fixed by time, place and geography and all the elements of a changing world. A practice regarded as decent in one period may be indecent in another."

Three years earlier this book had been on the Book-of-the-Month Club's selected list.

1954 *Madame Bovary* was on the blacklist of the National Organization of Decent Literature.

EDDY, MARY BAKER. (1821–1910)

1909 Boston: The Christian Science Church acquired and destroyed the plates and copies of Georgine Milmine's biography of Mrs. Eddy.

1927 The Church successfully suppressed Adam Dickey's *Memories of Mary Baker Eddy*.

1930 Scribner's resisted attempts of the Church to employ economic boycotts against Edwin F. Dakin's biography, *Mrs. Eddy, the Biography of a Virgin Mind*.

1931 The American Council of Learned Societies resisted Church pressure to withdraw the biography of Mrs. Eddy in the *Dictionary of American Biography*.

DUMAS ALEXANDRE, fils. (1824–1895)
La Dame aux Camélais, 1848.

1850 England-London: The authorities permitted the play's performance as an opera, *La Traviata;* but the translation of the text, as a libretto, was forbidden.

1852 France: After being forbidden on the Paris stage for three years, the play was produced through the efforts of Morny, the influential minister of Napoleon III.

1863 Italy-Rome: All love stories listed on the *Index.*

1958 Soviet Union: Works formerly banned reported to be extremely popular.

IBSEN, HENDRIK. (1828–1906)
Ghosts, 1881.

1881 Norway: The play, being a diagnosis of the diseases of modern society, and intended as a reform, was received with ill will.

1892 England: Application for license was refused by the Lord Chamberlain.

Long after Ibsen's position had been recognized in modern letters, the censor still interposed his shocked and obstinate personality between the British public and the great Norwegian author.

c.1915 Ban removed by the Lord Chamberlain.

1939 Spain: Works purged by the Franco government.

1958 Soviet Union: Works formerly banned reported to be extremely popular.

ROSSETTI, DANTE GABRIEL. (1828–1882)
Verses, 1847.

1833–46 Italy-Rome: Some of the author's poems, translated into Italian, were placed on the *Index.*

1871 England: Robert Buchanan, under the pseudoynm of "Thomas Maitland," in an article in the *Contemporary Review,* attacked Rossetti and the "fleshly school of poetry" as immoral, and one of his sonnets as "one profuse sweat of animalism." Rossetti, deeply hurt, replied in an article called "The Stealthy School of Criticism."

TOLSTOY, LEO. (1828–1910)
The Kreutzer Sonata, 1889.

1880 Russia: Various works forbidden publication were printed in Switzerland, England and Germany. In his early days, the writings of Tolstoy were greatly influenced by the philosophy of Rousseau, especially as expressed in *Émile.*

1890 United States: *The Kreutzer Sonata* was forbidden by the Post Office Department. In the ensuing controversy, Theodore Roosevelt denounced the author as a "sexual and moral pervert."

1926 Soviet Union: Many ethical works were banned or confined to the large libraries.
Hungary: All works banned.

1929 Italy: All works banned except in expensive editions.

1936 Soviet Union: Works topped the best seller list.

DODGSON, CHARLES L. (Lewis Carroll).
(1832–1898)
Alice's Adventures in Wonderland, 1865.

1931 China: Banned by the Governor of Hunan Province on the ground that "Animals should not use human language, and that it was disastrous to put animals and human beings on the same level."

CLEMENS, SAMUEL LANGHORNE (Mark Twain). (1835–1910)
The Adventures of Tom Sawyer, 1876.
The Adventures of Huckleberry Finn, 1885.

1876 United States-Brooklyn: *The Adventures of Tom Sawyer* was excluded from the children's room in the Public Library.

Denver: Excluded from the Public Library.

1885 Concord, Massachusetts: In the home town of Henry David Thoreau, *The Adventures of Huckleberry Finn* was banned by the Public Library as "trash and suitable only for the slums." The Concord Free Trade Club retaliated by electing the author to honorary membership.

1905 Brooklyn: The books were excluded from the children's room of the Public Library as bad examples for ingenuous youth. Asa Don Dickinson, Librarian of Brooklyn College, appealed to the author to defend the slander. His reply was not published until 1924 and said: "I am greatly troubled by what you say. I wrote *Tom Sawyer* and *Huck Finn* for adults exclusively, and it always distressed me when I find that boys and girls have been allowed access to them. The mind that becomes soiled in youth can never again be washed clean."

Note: Mrs. Clemens censored *Huckleberry Finn* and deleted the profanity and other strong passages, but left some which have at times been criticized, such as: "All kings is mostly rapscallions" (Chapter 23) and "so the king he blatted along" (Chapter 25). The London Athenaeum has called it one of the six greatest books ever written in America.

1930 Soviet Union: Books confiscated at the border.

1946 Books had become best sellers in the Soviet Union.

1957 United States-New York: Dropped from list of approved textbooks for senior and junior high schools.

GILBERT, W. S. (1836–1911)
and SULLIVAN, ARTHUR. (184⸺
H.M.S. Pinafore, 1878.
The Mikado, or the Town of Titipu⸺

c.1905 England: The British Foreign Off⸺
for, although *The Mikado* had b⸺
1885, and had been a great popu⸺
Chamberlain suddenly awoke to th⸺
in the piece, and forbade its furt⸺
ground that it might give offense t⸺
As a matter of fact, the music was b⸺
bands on Japanese ships on the M⸺
ban.

   Lewis Carroll (C. L. Dodgson)⸺
formance of *Pinafore* given by child⸺
"Damme, it's too bad," of the Cap ⸺
wrote: "I cannot find words to co⸺
pain I felt in seeing those dear child⸺
words to amuse ears grown callous."

WOODHULL, VICTORIA. (1836⸺
Woodhull and Claflin's Weekly, 187⸺

1872 United States: The November 2 issue⸺
of the private life of Henry Ward⸺
Plymouth Congregational Church in⸺
suppressed at the instance of Anthor⸺
ganized the New York Society for th⸺
the following year, for obscenity an⸺
editors were jailed.

SWINBURNE, ALGERNON CHA⸺
The Queen Mother, Rosamond—Tw⸺
Poems and Ballads, 1866.
The Devil's Due, 1875.

1860 England: *The Queen Mother* and R⸺
drawn from circulation because of str⸺
their alleged licentiousness.
1866 *Poems and Ballads* evoked a storm of⸺

CLEMENS, SAMUEL LANGHORNE (Mark Twain). (1835–1910)
The Adventures of Tom Sawyer, 1876.
The Adventures of Huckleberry Finn, 1885.

1876 United States-Brooklyn: *The Adventures of Tom Sawyer* was excluded from the children's room in the Public Library.

Denver: Excluded from the Public Library.

1885 Concord, Massachusetts: In the home town of Henry David Thoreau, *The Adventures of Huckleberry Finn* was banned by the Public Library as "trash and suitable only for the slums." The Concord Free Trade Club retaliated by electing the author to honorary membership.

1905 Brooklyn: The books were excluded from the children's room of the Public Library as bad examples for ingenuous youth. Asa Don Dickinson, Librarian of Brooklyn College, appealed to the author to defend the slander. His reply was not published until 1924 and said: "I am greatly troubled by what you say. I wrote *Tom Sawyer* and *Huck Finn* for adults exclusively, and it always distressed me when I find that boys and girls have been allowed access to them. The mind that becomes soiled in youth can never again be washed clean."

Note: Mrs. Clemens censored *Huckleberry Finn* and deleted the profanity and other strong passages, but left some which have at times been criticized, such as: "All kings is mostly rapscallions" (Chapter 23) and "so the king he blatted along" (Chapter 25). The London Athenaeum has called it one of the six greatest books ever written in America.

1930 Soviet Union: Books confiscated at the border.

1946 Books had become best sellers in the Soviet Union.

1957 United States-New York: Dropped from list of approved textbooks for senior and junior high schools.

GILBERT, W. S. (1836–1911)
and SULLIVAN, ARTHUR. (1842–1900)
H.M.S. Pinafore, 1878.
The Mikado, or the Town of Titipu, 1885.

c.1905 England: The British Foreign Office was much distressed for, although *The Mikado* had been first performed in 1885, and had been a great popular success, "The Lord Chamberlain suddenly awoke to the unsuspected dangers in the piece, and forbade its further production on the ground that it might give offense to our Japanese allies." As a matter of fact, the music was being played by Japanese bands on Japanese ships on the Medway River during the ban.

Lewis Carroll (C. L. Dodgson) earlier attended a performance of *Pinafore* given by children and of the famous "Damme, it's too bad," of the Captain and the chorus he wrote: "I cannot find words to convey to the reader the pain I felt in seeing those dear children taught to utter such words to amuse ears grown callous."

WOODHULL, VICTORIA. (1836–1927)
Woodhull and Claflin's Weekly, 1872.

1872 United States: The November 2 issue, containing an exposé of the private life of Henry Ward Beecher, minister of Plymouth Congregational Church in Brooklyn, N.Y., was suppressed at the instance of Anthony Comstock, who organized the New York Society for the Suppression of Vice the following year, for obscenity and libel. The feminist editors were jailed.

SWINBURNE, ALGERNON CHARLES. (1837–1909)
The Queen Mother, Rosamond—Two Plays, 1860.
Poems and Ballads, 1866.
The Devil's Due, 1875.

1860 England: *The Queen Mother* and *Rosamond* were withdrawn from circulation because of strenuous objections to their alleged licentiousness.

1866 *Poems and Ballads* evoked a storm of excitement over the author, whom Robert Buchanan classed with Rossetti and his circle as "the fleshly school." Swinburne's "hound of a publisher" became frightened and withdrew the book, which was later issued by John Hotten.

1875 *The Devil's Due,* an open letter to Buchanan, was immediately suppressed as libelous.

HARDY, THOMAS. (1840–1928)
Tess of the D'Urbervilles: A Pure Woman Faithfully Portrayed, 1891.
Jude the Obscure, 1895.

c.1891 England: *Tess* was banned by the circulating libraries (*q.v.*) which held a virtual censorship over popular reading. United States-Boston: Highly disapproved by the Watch and Ward Society.

1896 England: *Jude the Obscure* banned by the circulating libraries.

ZOLA, ÉMILE. (1840–1902)
Nana, 1880.
La Terre, 1887.
J'Accuse, 1898.

1888 England: Vizetelly, the publisher, was imprisoned for publishing *La Terre* although, ironically, it was the expurgated editions of Zola's novels that so outraged the Victorian era.

1894 Italy-Rome: All Zola's works were placed on the *Index.*

1898 France: Zola caused a judicial inquiry to be made into the notorious Dreyfus affair which was convulsing French politics and society, and published the open letter, *J'Accuse,* in *L'Aurore.* It was a strong denunciation of all who, on the slightest evidence, had convicted Dreyfus of selling military secrets, had banished him to Devil's Island, and had refused all appeals for a new trial. Zola, condemned for libel of the army chiefs, escaped to England, where the publisher of his "pernicious novels" had been jailed. Anatole France said "his work is evil and he is one of those unhappy beings of whom one could say that it would be better had he never been born."

1929 Yugoslavia: All works banned.
1953 Ireland: All works banned.
1954 United States: *Nana* disapproved by the National Organization of Decent Literature.

EXTRACTS PRINCIPALLY FROM ENGLISH CLASSICS: Showing that the Legal Suppression of M. Zola's Novels Would Logically Involve the Bowdlerizing of Some of the Greatest Works in English Literature.
Compiled by and privately printed for Henry Vizetelly, 1888.

1888 England-London: This volume is in defense of Vizetelly, publisher and champion of Flaubert, Goncourt, Gautier, Maupassant, Daudet and Longfellow. Although a sick old man, Vizetelly was sentenced to prison for publishing such "pernicious literature" as the novels of Zola, and died shortly after his release.

FRANCE, ANATOLE (Jacques Anatole Thibault).
(1844–1924)
A Mummer's Tale, 1921.

1921 Sweden: Author awarded the Nobel prize for literature.
1922 Italy-Rome: The *Index* placed its most stringent prohibition on the reading of the works of France by listing simply and conclusively *Opera Omnia.*
1953 Ireland: *A Mummer's Tale* banned.

MAUPASSANT, HENRI RENÉ ALBERT GUY de.
(1850–1893)
Des Vers, 1880.
Une Vie: L'Humble Vérité, 1883.

1880 France: Legal proceedings against *Des Vers* were withdrawn through the influence of Senator Cordier. Flaubert, the teacher of Maupassant, who had been prosecuted for *Madame Bovary,* congratulated his pupil on the similarity of their literary experiences.
1883 The sale of *Une Vie* was forbidden at railway bookstalls.

The prohibition drew much attention to the master of the short story.

1930 Canada: Many of this author's works were on the blacklist of the Customs Office.

MOORE, GEORGE. (1852–1933)
Flowers of Passion, 1878.
A Modern Lover, 1883.
A Mummer's Wife, 1885.
Esther Waters, 1894.
A Story Teller's Holiday, 1918.

c.1878 Ireland: Edmund Yates called the author of *Flowers of Passion* a "bestial bard," and advised whipping him and burning the book.

1883 England: *A Modern Lover,* a three-volume novel, was banned by Mudie's Circulating Library, which exercised a virtual censorship because every one borrowed, and few bought, the expensive three-volume novels of the day. Moore vowed revenge and published his next novel, *A Mummer's Wife,* in an inexpensive single volume, thereby starting a vogue to break the monopoly of circulating libraries.

1894 Circulating libraries refused to stock *Esther Waters.*

1929 United States: The Customs refused admittance to *A Story Teller's Holiday.* The officer who seized the copy, which contained the author's autograph, vandalized it by marking out offending passages.

   This incident, together with the banning of *Lady Chatterley's Lover,* touched off a lengthy and often acrimonious debate in the United States Senate which led finally to some easing of the regulations of the U.S. Customs. This reform in turn precipitated the famous decision to allow Joyce's *Ulysses* (*q.v.*) into the United States.

1932 The Customs Court judged it obscene.

1933 The Treasury Department admitted it as a modern classic.

   George Moore once remarked that if all the books objected to by censors as sexually stimulating were swept from the face of the earth, the spring breeze would still remain to awaken desires in man and woman.

HARRIS, FRANK. (1855–1931)
My Life and Loves, 4 vols., 1922–1927.

1922 England: Banned. Not published in that country until 1938.

1925 United States-New York: The Society for the Suppression of Vice, under John S. Sumner, seized about 300 copies of the second volume and prosecuted Harris' New York agent, who eventually was sentenced to ninety days in the workhouse.

SHAW, GEORGE BERNARD. (1856–1950)
Mrs. Warren's Profession, 1898.
Man and Superman, 1903.
The Shewing-up of Blanco Posnet, 1909.
The Adventures of the Black Girl in her Search for God, 1932.

1905 United States-New York: The New York Public Library withdrew *Man and Superman* from the public shelves to reserve judgment, and Anthony Comstock complained to Arnold Daly, producer of *Mrs. Warren's Profession,* which had been suppressed in London and called it "reekings." Shaw, infuriated, coined the word "Comstockery." Comstock retaliated and took arms against "this Irish smut-dealer's books." *Mrs. Warren's Profession* was taken to court, where it was held not actionable. The Comstock publicity greatly increased the attendance at the stage production; police reserves were called out on opening night to dispel the crowds. One newspaper critic referred to the play as "tainted drama" and another, fearful of the word "prostitution," accused it of having "an unspeakable theme." The play soon closed.

1909 England-London: The Lord Chamberlain refused a license for performance of *The Shewing-up of Blanco Posnet.* Shaw thereupon wrote a statement, privately printed, for submission to a parliamentary committee of inquiry. In its published report, the Committee deliberately omitted Shaw's remarks, whereupon Shaw made them the preface to the published version of the play.

1925 Sweden-Stockholm: Shaw was awarded the Nobel prize for literature.

1929 Yugoslavia: All works banned from the public libraries.

1933 England: *The Adventures of the Black Girl in her Search for God* was banned from the Cambridge Public Library.

1939 Italy: Shaw, informed that his works and those of Shakespeare were the only English books exempted by the Propaganda Ministry from the sanctions reprisals, replied that he was greatly flattered to be in such good company.

WILDE, OSCAR FINGAL O'FLAHERTIE WILLS.
(1856–1900)
Salomé, 1893.

1892 England: The play was being rehearsed in London by Sarah Bernhardt when the Lord Chamberlain withheld its license on the ground that the play introduced biblical characters. The *London Times* called it "an arrangement in blood and ferocity; morbid, bizarre, repulsive and very often offensive in its adaptation of scriptural phraseology to situations and the reverse of sacred."

1895 France: Played by Sarah Bernhardt.
United States-Boston: Banned in book form.

1907 Boston: The New England Watch and Ward Society prevented Mary Garden from appearing in Richard Strauss' celebrated opera *Salomé* and banned the performance.

OBSCENE PUBLICATIONS ACT. (1859–1930)

1857 England: This law, enacted at the urging of Lord Chief Justice Campbell, who was incensed by Dumas' *The Lady of the Camellias,* established the ground upon which obscenity convictions were obtained in England and the United States in the following century. It was a particularly troublesome law because it provided for the seizure of materials under a general search warrant, and put the burden of proof upon the accused. While it did not alter the existing common law on the definition of obscene libel, it provided the means of forestalling sales through early seizure and destruction.

1868 The significant change in legal emphasis came in this year when Lord Chief Justice Cockburn enunciated the so-called

Hicklin doctrine: "The test of obscenity is this, whether the tendency of the matter charged as obscenity is to deprave and corrupt those whose minds are open to such immoral influences and into whose hands a publication of this sort may fall."

1873 United States: The Comstock Act was enacted by the U.S. Congress with effects similar to those of the English law. While the Comstock Act has never been repealed, its effect has been eroded by recent court decisions.

1959 England: A new act replaced the 102-year old law of 1857. Its liberal provisions include the now generally accepted doctrine that a work must be considered in its entirety, and that if a work can be proved to have merit, any incidental obscenities become irrelevant. The law also provides for the taking of expert testimony.

DOYLE, SIR ARTHUR CONAN. (1859–1930)
The Adventures of Sherlock Holmes, 1892.

1929 Soviet Union: Banned because of its references to occultism and spiritualism.

ELLIS, HAVELOCK. (1859–1939)
Studies in the Psychology of Sex, 1897–1910.

1887 England-London: As editor of the Mermaid series of British dramatists, Ellis issued the first volume, on Christopher Marlowe, which reproduced a document that had been used against the Elizabethan playwright. Because of protests the publisher, Vizetelly, suppressed some of the offending language in subsequent reprints. After Vizetelly was disgraced for publishing Zola's works, Fisher Unwin took over the Mermaid series, dismissed Ellis and further bowdlerized the texts that Ellis had prepared.

1898 England-London: *Studies in the Psychology of Sex* was condemned as "lewd, wicked, bawdy, scandalous and obscene," and the prosecution raised a storm of protest. Ellis was not allowed to defend the scientific nature of his work in court, so he formed a Defense Committee including George Bernard Shaw, George Moore and others. The first publisher willing to sponsor the books proved to be dishonest, was arrested, took poison said to be hidden in his ring, and died. A copy of the first volume under a Leipzig imprint was bought by the police from G. Bedborough, who was arrested but later released on turning State's evidence. The second volume was seized and burned. It was barred from the library of the British Museum. Ellis resolved to publish the subsequent volumes outside England.

1901 United States-Philadelphia: F. A. Davis Company, medical publishers, issued the seven volumes for sale to physicians only.

It was not until after Joyce's *Ulysses* had been cleared in court that the *Studies* were offered to the general public and also became available in England, where the Royal Society of Physicians made Ellis a fellow.

1953 Ireland: Banned.

MAETERLINCK, MAURICE. (1862–1949)
Monna Vanna, 1902.

1909 England: *Monna Vanna* was censored by the Lord Chamberlain as improper for the stage, asserting, "Our decision was almost universally upheld."

1914 Italy-Rome: All works listed on the *Index*.

1926 Soviet Union: Works restricted to the large libraries.

SCHNITZLER, ARTHUR. (1862–1931)
Reigen, 1900.
Casanova's Homecoming, 1918.

1924 United States: The English translation of *Casanova's Homecoming* was indicted as obscene. The indictment was attacked, whereupon Judge Wagner maintained that the book was sufficiently corrupting for the indictment to stand, his point being: "We may assert with pride, though not boastfully, that we are essentially an idealistic and spiritual nation, and exact a higher standard than some others." The publisher withheld publication and the case was not tried. Meanwhile the book circulated freely in the original German.

1929 New York: A bookseller was convicted by the Court of Special Sessions for selling a copy of *Reigen.* The Appellate Division upheld the conviction, basing their decision more on the "exquisite handling of the licentious" described in the introduction rather than the text. Since the book had been pirated and privately printed, the author was in complete ignorance of the introduction. The conviction was sustained by the highest state court. Shortly afterwards *Reigen,* which had been studied widely in college and university courses in German literature, was published by the Modern Library, and no further attempt was made to suppress it. *Reigen* had been played abroad since 1903.

1930 John S. Sumner, secretary of the New York Society for the Suppression of Vice, brought Simon and Schuster to court for publishing *Casanova's Homecoming.* The case was dismissed.

1939 Italy: *Casanova's Homecoming* was banned by Mussolini.

D'ANNUNZIO, GABRIELE. (1863–1938)
Writings, 1880–c. 1900.

1898 United States-Boston: *The Triumph of Death,* 1894, was brought to court by the Watch and Ward Society, but not convicted.

1911 Italy-Rome: All love stories and plays placed on the *Index.*

1926 Rome: In spite of the fact that many of D'Annunzio's works were on the *Index,* the Italian Government voted to publish them in a deluxe edition. D'Annunzio's admirers subscribed 6,000,000 lire for the purpose.

1928 While the author lived at Lake Garda, enshrined as Italy's beloved patriot and poet, the *Index* further prohibited his mystic poetry and mystery plays.

1935 Autobiography banned by Mussolini.

1936 Rome: The Government Tourist Bureau postponed indefinitely the presentation of D'Annunzio's play *The Martyrdom of Saint Sebastion.* The Bishop of Pompeii highly disapproved of it and forbade all Catholics to attend.

1937 Appointed president of the Royal Italian Academy by Mussolini.

1938 After the death of the great patriot, the catafalque was covered with the trophies of his campaigns and included a semi-official statement from the Vatican denying the widespread impression that he had been excommunicated.

Mussolini and members of his Cabinet joined the thousands of mourners at the bier.

GLYN, ELINOR. (1865?–1943)
Three Weeks, 1907.

1907 England-London: The book was banned as immoral.
Canada: Sale forbidden on government trains.

1908 United States-Boston: A representative of the publisher was arrested for selling a copy of the novel, and was held on bail. The action was instituted by the Watch and Ward Society, which submitted copies of the book to the District Attorney and the judges of the lower court. Referred to the Grand Jury, whose indictment said that "the language on certain pages of the book is improper to be placed upon the court records and offensive to the court."

KIPLING, RUDYARD. (1865–1936)
A Fleet in Being: Notes of Two Trips With the Channel Squadron, 1898.

1898 England: Suppressed on grounds that the book betrayed naval secrets, although the author was well known as an intense patriot.

WELLS, H. G. (1866–1946)
The World of William Clissold, 1926.

1929 United States-Boston: Banned.

PHILLIPS, DAVID GRAHAM. (1867–1911)
Susan Lenox, 1917.

1917 New York: Attacked by John S. Sumner, the publisher, D. Appleton, was prepared to defend in court this novel about a prostitute who rises to respectability. However, the author's sister and literary executor persuaded the publisher to remove the offending passages.

PRZYBSZKEWSKI, STANISLAW. (1868–1927)
Homo Sapiens, 1915.

1915 United States-New York: Brought before magistrate's court by John S. Sumner, Alfred Knopf was charged with publishing an obscene book. Knopf yielded to pressure, withdrew the book and melted down the plates.

DIMNET, ABBÉ ERNEST. (1869–1954)
La Pensée Catholique dans l'Angleterre Contemporaine, 1905.

1907 Italy-Rome: Listed on the *Index.*

GIDE, ANDRÉ PAUL GUILLAUME. (1869–1951)
If It Die, 1926.

1935 United States-New York: An officer of the Gotham Book Mart was arrested by a patrolman who had bought *If It Die* and taken it to John S. Sumner, who considered some of the passages obscene. At the time the book was taken to court 100,000 copies had been sold in France and Germany, and the limited edition of 1500 copies published in America had been sold out.

1936 Magistrate Nathan D. Perlman said in his decision that the author had "unveiled the darker corners of his life," but he held that "the book as a complete entity was not obscene" and dismissed the case.

1938 Soviet Union: Gide incurred a Soviet ban on his works following his split with Communism.

1952 Italy-Rome: Although a Nobel prize winner, all the author's works were placed on the *Index.*

1953 Ireland: *If It Die* banned.

1954 Germany-East Berlin: Writings forbidden by the Soviet occupation authorities.

LENIN, VLADIMIR ILYICH (Ulyanov).
(1870–1924)
The State and Revolution, 1917.
Proletarian Revolution in Russia, 1918.

1927 United States-Boston: *The State and Revolution* was seized as obscene.

Hungary: Seized as subversive.

1928 Canada: *Proletarian Revolution in Russia* burned by the authorities.

1940 United States-Oklahoma City: A vigilante organization made an unofficial raid on the bookshop of Robert Wood, State Secretary of the Communist party, and seized many books, including *The State and Revolution,* Communist literature, works of fiction and economics, *The Declaration of Independence* and the *Constitution of the United States.* These books were publicly burned at the City Stadium. Mr. and Mrs. Wood, customers in the shop and a carpenter repairing shelves were arrested on charges of criminal syndicalism and held incommunicado. Of the eighteen arrested, six were held as witnesses. Mr. Wood was charged with distributing literature advocating violence, and Mrs. Wood and two others with belonging to the Communist party. All six were sentenced to ten years in prison and fined $5,000, the only evidence being books and pamphlets relating to the party. There was no attempt to show that the defendants had committed an overt act against the government, or were guilty of anything except selling books. No witnesses for the defense were permitted. The convictions were protested by many organizations, publishers and writers.

1943 The Court of Appeals reversed the convictions.

1954 Providence, R.I.: The local post office attempted to withhold from delivery to Brown University seventy-five copies of *The State and Revolution* as "subversive."

LOUŸS, PIERRE. (1870–1925)
The Songs of Bilitis, 1894.
Aphrodite, 1896.
The Twilight of the Nymphs, 1903.

1929 United States: *Aphrodite* banned by the Customs Department as lascivious, corrupting and obscene, as well as *The Songs of Bilitis* and *The Twilight of the Nymphs.*

1930 New York: E. B. Marks, book dealer, was fined $250 for possessing a copy of *Aphrodite,* in violation of the State laws against objectionable literature.

1935 The importation of copies of *Aphrodite* was forbidden in a deluxe edition, although a forty-nine cent copy was freely advertised in the *New York Times Book Review,* and delivered for ten cents extra through the United States mails.

1954 *Aphrodite* condemned by the National Organization of Decent Literature, and other local censorship groups throughout the country.

DREISER, THEODORE. (1871–1945)
Sister Carrie, 1900.
The Genius, 1915.
An American Tragedy, 1925.
Dawn, 1931.

1900 United States-New York: *Sister Carrie* printed by Doubleday. An undetermined number of advance copies were released before the publisher's wife objected. The remainder of the edition was suppressed. Although an English edition appeared in 1901, the American public did not have ready access to this modern classic until the second edition in 1907.

1916 New York: *The Genius* was suppressed.

1923 *The Genius* was republished; the jacket blurb flaunted the fact that the volume had been suppressed by the New York Society for the Suppression of Vice.

1930 Boston: The Superior Court condemned *An American Tragedy* and fined the publisher $300, but across the Charles River it was required reading for a Harvard English course.

1932 Ireland: *Dawn* was banned.

1933 Germany: *The Genius* and *An American Tragedy* were burned by the Nazis because "they deal with low love affairs."

1935 United States-Boston: *An American Tragedy* still banned, though obtainable by mail.

1953 Ireland: *Dawn* still banned.

1958 United States-Vermont: *Sister Carrie* still banned.

RASPUTIN, GRIGORI YEFIMOVICH. (1871–1916)
My Thoughts and Meditations, 1915.

1915 Russia: In the preface the editors commented on the author's meteoric rise from lowly peasant origin. He resented this and forced it to be deleted from the book.

DENNETT, MARY WARE. (1872–1947)
The Sex Side of Life, an Explanation for Young People, 1918.

1922 United States-New York: Originally written for the instruction of Mrs. Dennett's sons, the pamphlet was declared unmailable by the Post Office Department, although it was published four years earlier by the *Medical Review of Reviews,* and was widely used by the Y.M.C.A., Union Theological Seminary, government hospitals and others.

1928 Mrs. Dennett received a request for the pamphlet from a "Mrs. Miles" in Virginia. The lady turned out to be a postal inspector who had been instructed to trap the author.

1929 Author tried and sentenced by jury to a $300 fine for sending obscene matter through the mails.

1930 Conviction reversed on appeal.

RUSSELL, BERTRAND. (1872–1970)
What I Believe, 1925.

1929 United States-Boston: Banned.

1940 Russell was appointed Professor of Philosophy at the College of the City of New York. Bishop William T. Manning of the Episcopal Church denounced the appointment because Russell was a "recognized propagandist against religion and morality." A Brooklyn housewife instituted suit against the Board of Higher Education on the ground that her daughter might be injured if she enrolled in one of Russell's classes. The Court supported the woman's suit, and Russell's appointment was voided. Despite a national outcry of protest, New York authorities refused to appeal the decision.

LA MOTTE, ELLEN N. (1873–1961)
The Backwash of War, 1916.

1919 England: Suppressed for its pacifistic thesis.

SIMKHOVITCH, VLADIMIR G. (1874–1959)
Marxism Versus Socialism, 1913.

1917 Soviet Union: The Russian translation was burned at the outbreak of the Revolution. It is now unprocurable; but the volume is available in French, German, Italian, English, and Japanese.

AMERICAN LIBRARY ASSOCIATION
(organized 1876)

1918 The American Library Association, which had undertaken to administer the book program for soldiers, was chastised by the War Department for permitting the inclusion in servicemen's libraries of Ambrose Bierce's *In the Midst of Life* and Henri Barbusse's *Under Fire,* a prize-winning French novel. The ALA thereupon withdrew these books from its program.

ANDERSON, SHERWOOD. (1874–1959)
Many Marriages, 1922.
Horses and Men, 1923.
Dark Laughter, 1925.

1923 England: *Many Marriages* aroused legal action.
1930 United States-Boston: *Dark Laughter* was blacklisted.
1931 Ireland: *Horses and Men* banned.

LONDON, JACK. (1876–1916)
The Call of the Wild, 1903.

1929 Italy: All cheap editions were banned.
Yugoslavia: All works banned as too radical.

1932 Germany: Various works were cast into the Nazi bonfires.

SINCLAIR, UPTON. (1878–1968)
The Jungle, 1906.
Oil!, 1927.
No Pasarán, 1937.
Wide Is the Gate, 1943.

1910 United States: A campaign was started to ban *The Jungle,* but it was unsuccessful.

1927 Boston: *Oil!* was forbidden because of its comments on the Harding administration. The author defended the case himself and addressed a crowd of 2,000 on Boston Common on the character and aim of his book. The nine pages objected to, including the two pages quoted from the *Song of Solomon,* were deleted by a large black fig leaf. The bookseller was fined $100, and the trial cost the author $2,000.

1929 Yugoslavia: All works banned by the public libraries.

1933 Germany: Works burned in the Nazi bonfires because of Sinclair's socialist views.

1938 South Africa-Johannesburg: *No Pasarán,* a book against fascism in Spain, banned.

1953 Ireland: *Wide Is the Gate* banned.

1956 East Germany-Berlin: Sinclair's works banned as inimical to Communism.

CABELL, JAMES BRANCH. (1879–1958)
Jurgen, A Comedy of Justice, 1919.
The Devil's Own Dear Son, 1949.

1920 United States: *Jurgen* was prosecuted by the New York Society for the Suppression of Vice. Several hundred people prominent in public and literary life presented petitions protesting against the action. This publicity established a hitherto obscure novel as a best seller.

1922 Although indicted as obscene two years before, the book was now deemed a "work of art," and the indictment was dismissed.

1935 Volume unobtainable in many large public libraries.

1953 Ireland: *Jurgen* and *The Devil's Own Dear Son* banned.

TROTSKY, LEON (Bronstein). **(1879–1940)**
Second Congress of the Russian Socialist Democratic Workers' Party: Report of the Siberian Delegation, 1903.

1903 Russia: *Report* banned by the Imperial Government.

1927 Soviet Union: Banned by the Government. Therefore the same writings were banned by two opposing ideologies for the same reason—that they opposed the existing philosophies of government.

1930 United States-Boston: Works banned.

1933 Germany: All works banned.
Soviet Union: All works banned.

1934 Italy: All works banned except in deluxe editions.

ASCH, SHOLEM. **(1880–1957)**
The God of Vengeance, 1923.

1923 United States-New York: Asch's play was closed by police and the leading performer was fined.

NOYES, ALFRED. **(1880–1958)**
Voltaire, 1936.

1938 England: Noyes, a Roman Catholic, was denounced to the Holy Office for his biography of Voltaire. The volume was withdrawn by the publishers and revised to meet the demands of the censors.

STOPES, MARIE CARMICHAEL. **(1880–1958)**
Wise Parenthood, 1918.
Married Love, 1918.
Contraception: Its Theory, History and Practice, 1923.
Vestia, 1926.

1918 England: On publication, *Wise Parenthood* was made a notorious test case.

Canada: Prohibited.

England: 700,000 copies of *Married Love* were sold.

1921 United States-New York State: A physician was convicted for selling a copy of *Married Love.*

1930 *Contraception* was refused entry by the U.S. Customs, but after vindication the case cleared the way for future importation of birth control literature.

1931 New York: Ban on *Married Love* raised by Judge John M. Woolsey. His decision was: "I cannot imagine a normal mind to which this book would seem to be obscene or immoral within the proper definition of those words, or whose sex impulses would be stirred by reading it. . . . Instead of being inhospitably received it should, I think, be welcomed within our borders."

Customs ban raised on *Married Love.*

Ireland: All works banned.

England: The Lord Chamberlain refused to license *Vestia* for the stage, although it was legally circulated in book form.

1939 United States: After the sale of one million copies of *Married Love,* it was published in a forty-nine cent reprint.

Ireland: *Married Love* banned in English.

1953 Ireland: All works banned.

JOYCE, JAMES. (1882–1941)
Dubliners, 1914.
Ulysses, 1922.

1912 Ireland-Dublin: After years of delay and wrangling, *Dubliners* was printed in an edition of 1,000 copies. All but one copy was destroyed by the printer, John Falconer, because he found passages objectionable.

1914 *Dubliners* finally published.

1918 United States: Early installments of *Ulysses,* appearing in *The Little Review* (*q.v.*), were burned by the Post Office Department.

1922 Imported copies burned.

Ireland: Burned.

Canada: Burned.

1923 England: 499 copies burned by the Customs authorities at Folkstone.

United States: 500 copies burned by the Post Office Department. The court ruled against its publication. Consequently, there being no copyright, Joyce, who was becoming blind, did not benefit by the royalties of the thousands of pirated and bowdlerized editions.

1929 England: Banned.

1930 United States-New York: A copy of *Ulysses* sent to Random House was seized by the Collector of Customs as obscene, although this book had for more than a decade won enthusiastic critical acclaim and had profoundly influenced literature.

1933 New York: A copy addressed to Alexander Lindey, mailed from Paris was detained by the Customs. Lindey petitioned the Treasury Department to admit *Ulysses* as a classic, which they did, under Tariff Act provision which permits entry of so-called classics for noncommercial purposes at the discretion of the Secretary of Treasury.

The book was taken to court and defended by Morris L. Ernst. The ban was raised by Judge John M. Woolsey in a notable decision: "A rather strong draught . . . emetic, rather than aphrodisiac . . . a sincere and honest book . . . I do not detect anywhere the leer of a sensualist."

On appeal, United States Attorney Martin Conboy tried to convict the book on irreligious instead of obscene grounds, contending that "whatever constituted a reflection on the Church was indecent." Judge Woolsey's decision was upheld by a vote of two to one in an opinion written by Judge Augustus N. Hand.

Henry Seidel Canby said: "Its indecency would have appalled Rabelais and frightened Chaucer; but such a book is valuable in a world trying to be sane, trying to save itself by humor or insight from the perversion of honest instincts and from mental confusion only because of its new and brilliant technique, and the passages of undoubted genius."

This book has been translated into many languages and is on the reading lists of the English courses of many universities. It is considered one of the masterworks of the twentieth century.

1960 A Caedmon recording of the soliloquies of Leopold and Molly Bloom was bowdlerized.

1967 A film version of *Ulysses* was severely criticized in the United States for its frankness.

MACKENZIE, COMPTON. (1882–)
Sinister Street, 1913–14.

1913 England: Banned by circulating libraries (*q.v.*).

GOODMAN, DANIEL CARSON. (1883–1957)
Hagar Revelly, 1913.

1914 United States-New York: Although *Hagar Revelly* was written by a social hygienist hoping to instruct the young in the dangers of vice, it was attacked by Anthony Comstock. The publisher was acquitted after a brief trial in Federal Court. The importance of this case lay in the opinion of Judge Learned Hand, which contained the first serious legal challenge to the Hicklin Rule.

SANGER, MARGARET. (1883–1966)
Family Limitation, 1915.
Happiness in Marriage, 1926.
My Fight for Birth Control, 1931.

1915 United States-New York: *Family Limitation* was brought to court by the New York Society for the Suppression of Vice and found to be "contrary not only to the law of the state, but to the law of God," and Mrs. Sanger was jailed. William Sanger was jailed for thirty days for distributing his wife's pamphlets on birth control.

1923 England-London: The book was suppressed.

1929 United States-New York: On complaint of a chapter of the Daughters of the American Revolution to the Police Commissioner, Mrs. Sanger's clinic was raided. Three nurses and two doctors were arrested and carried off in a patrol wagon, along with thousands of case histories. Defended by five eminent physicians in a crowded courtroom, the case was dismissed. Representatives of the Academy of Medicine declared that there had been unwarranted interference with the freedom of physicians engaged in their lawful practice and warned against further interference.

1931 Ireland: Pamphlets banned.
Italy: Pamphlets banned.
Yugoslavia: Pamphlets banned.
United States-Boston: *My Fight for Birth Control* was omitted from the collection of the public library.

1950 Japan-Tokyo: Mrs. Sanger was refused permission by General MacArthur to enter the country for a lecture tour. The General was quoted as saying that birth control was a matter for the Japanese people and the Occupation had a policy of hands off.

1953 Ireland: *Happiness in Marriage* and *My Fight for Birth Control* banned.

1954 Japan-Tokyo: Mrs. Sanger, speaking on birth control, became the first woman from the United States to testify before the Japanese Diet.

FEUCHTWANGER, LION. (1884–1958)
Power, 1926.

1914–19 Germany: Works constantly suppressed during the war.
1930 United States-Boston: *Power* was banned for immorality.
1933 Germany: All works were burned in the Nazi bonfires. The author was exiled and his property confiscated.

DURANT, WILL. (1885–)
The Case for India, 1930.

1931 India: Banned, with many other pro-Gandhi books, by the British Viceroy of India.

LAWRENCE, DAVID HERBERT. (1885–1930)
Sons and Lovers, 1913.
The Rainbow, 1915.
Women in Love, 1920.
Lady Chatterley's Lover, 1928.
The Paintings of D. H. Lawrence, 1929.
Love Among the Haystacks, 1930.
The First Lady Chatterley, 1944.

1915 England-London: Under Lord Campbell's Act of 1857, over 1,000 copies of the first edition of *The Rainbow* were ordered destroyed by the magistrate's court. As a result, the book was not republished in England until 1926, in expurgated form. The full text did not appear again until 1949.

1922 United States: *Women in Love* seized by John S. Sumner of the New York Society for the Suppression of Vice. The case was dismissed in court, but the countersuit for libel was sustained.

1929 *Lady Chatterley's Lover* and *Collected Paintings* were barred by Customs.
England: *The Rainbow,* freely circulated in America, was banned, while *Women in Love* was not objected to.

1930 United States-Washington, D.C.: *Lady Chatterley's Lover* had prominence in the famed "decency debates" in the Senate between Senator Bronson Cutting of New Mexico, who was in favor of modifying the censorship laws, and Senator Reed Smoot of Utah, who was against it. Cutting enraged Smoot by witty insinuations that *Lady Chatterley* was a favorite with the Mormon Senator.

1932 Ireland: *Lady Chatterley's Lover* banned.
Poland: *Lady Chatterley's Lover* banned.

1944 United States-New York: John S. Sumner appeared at the offices of the Dial Press with a search warrant and seized 400 copies of *The First Lady Chatterley.* It is the first version of *Lady Chatterley's Lover,* published in the twenties in Italy, but not issued in its entirety in America before. Magistrate Charles G. Keutgen declared the book obscene and committed the case for trial in the Court of Special Sessions, where it was exonerated by two of the three judges and the case dismissed.

1953 England: *Lady Chatterley's Lover* was removed from the shelves of two retail establishments as being obscene. The magistrate hearing the case declared it "absolute rubbish" and said had he read the unexpurgated edition he would have chucked it on the fire.

1953 United States: *Lady Chatterley* and *Love Among the Haystacks* were on the blacklist of the National Organization of Decent Literature.

1959 United States-New York: Grove Press published the unexpurgated edition of *Lady Chatterley's Lover,* copies of which were seized by the Post Office and impounded. Challenged in court, the Post Office seizure was overturned.

During the succeeding years the novel was banned in several nations, including Australia, Japan, and India. A film based on the novel was also widely attacked.

1960 England-London: Penguin Books published the unexpurgated edition, which was challenged by the Director of Public Prosecutions under the Obscene Publications Act of the previous year. A lengthy trial ensued, which itself became the subject of a book. The jury returned a "not guilty" verdict, thus freeing Lawrence's novel after more than thirty years of litigation, piracy, smuggling and suppression.

1960 Canada-Montreal: Banned by court order. Ban lifted by the Supreme Court in 1962.

1961 Canada: Customs held up the import of *The Trial of Lady Chatterley,* which was itself not obscene, but was merely a detailed report of the court case involving Lawrence's novel.

LEWIS, SINCLAIR. (1885–1951)
Elmer Gantry, 1927.
Ann Vickers, 1933.
It Can't Happen Here, 1935.
Cass Timberlane, 1945.
Kingsblood Royal, 1947.

1927 United States-Boston: *Elmer Gantry* was banned because a religious hero was depicted as obscene. The publishers defended the suit and expressed their amazement at the discretionary powers invested in local officials.

Washington, D.C.: The Post Office Department upheld postmasters as censors.

Banned by the libraries of Camden, New Jersey; Glasgow, Scotland; and others.

1930 Sweden-Stockholm: Lewis was the first American to be awarded the Nobel prize for literature.

1931 Ireland: *Elmer Gantry* was banned as offensive to public morals.

United States-New York: The Post Office Department banned any catalogue listing the book.

1936 Hollywood: A storm was aroused by the refusal of a moving picture company to film the anti-fascist novel *It Can't Happen Here*. Lewis accused Will Hays, head of the motion picture industry, of forbidding the production. Hays replied that the decision had been made by the producing company. In the meantime there was a storm of protest from the press and the controversy doubled the sale of the book.

1938 Massachusetts-Cohasset: Lewis appeared in a revised version of the play *It Can't Happen Here,* playing the part of Doremus Jessup.

1953 Illinois: *Kingsblood Royal* was one of the 6,000 books "relating to sex" which were removed from state libraries on the complaint of a mother who claimed that her daughter had borrowed a book that was offensive.
Ireland: *Ann Vickers, Cass Timberlane* and *Elmer Gantry* banned.

1954 Germany-East Berlin: Works banned.

HALL, RADCLYFFE. (1886–1943)
The Well of Loneliness, 1928.

1928 England-London: Withdrawn from sale by the publisher at the request of the Home Office, followed by contradictory decisions of several courts and much controversy. Among those who protested the suppression of the novel were George Bernard Shaw, Laurence Housman, Rose Macaulay, John Buchan, Lytton Strachey, Laurence Binyon and others.

1929 United States-New York: John S. Sumner, Secretary of the New York Society for the Suppression of Vice, acting under a warrant issued by Chief Magistrate McAdoo, raided the office of the publisher and removed 865 copies remaining from the sixth edition, then raided Macy's book department.

1939 New York: The book, defended by Morris L. Ernst, was finally cleared. The case was significant because the judge sought to inject a new element into the obscenity law in declaring the subject matter, rather than words or phrases, "offensive to decency."

1944 Miss Hall received the Femina Vie Heureuse Prize and the James Tait Black Prize for her novel, *Adam's Breed.*

The New York *Herald-Tribune* wrote: "*The Well of Loneliness* is much more of a sermon than a story, a passionate plea for the world's understanding and sympathy, as much a novel of problem and purpose as *Uncle Tom's Cabin,* as sentimental and moralistic as the deepest-dyed of the Victorians."

CLARKE, DONALD HENDERSON. (1887–1958)
Female, 1933.

1933 United States-New York: Criminal proceedings for obscenity were brought in Manhattan against the publisher of *Female.* However, the judge dismissed the complaint.

Five months later, a clerk in an Astoria, Long Island, lending library rented a copy of the novel to a police officer and was subsequently served with a summons and held for trial. The defendant was found guilty of renting an obscene book and sentenced to a fine of $100 or twenty days in jail.

O'NEILL, EUGENE. (1888–1953)
Desire Under the Elms, 1924.
Strange Interlude, 1928.

1925 United States-New York: *Desire Under the Elms* was closed by New York police.

1928 New York: *Strange Interlude* opened and brought the playwright his third Pulitzer Prize.

1929 Massachusetts: *Strange Interlude* was banned in Boston but performed in Quincy. The censorship was supported by the influential Catholic paper, *The Pilot,* but attacked by the secular press.

1936 Sweden-Stockholm: O'Neill awarded the Nobel prize for literature.

HITLER, ADOLF. (1889–1945)
Mein Kampf, 1925–7.

1932 Germany: The authorized translation was considerably abridged for foreign consumption.

Czechoslovakia: Banned for its fierce militaristic doctrines.

1936 United States-New York: A first edition containing many passages suppressed later was sold at the American Art Association Anderson Galleries for $250. It was the first time the book had been sold at auction on either side of the Atlantic and the first time that police protection had been needed at an American book auction. Threats of a demonstration during the sale caused Mr. Parke to send for the police.

1937 Palestine: Once banned, the testament became a best seller among the Arabs.

CONNELLY, MARC. (1890–)
The Green Pastures, 1929.

1929 England: The play was forbidden on the ground that the Deity ought not to be represented on the stage.
United States: Awarded the Pulitzer Prize.

1933 Norway: Forbidden to be played in the National Theatre.

PASTERNAK, BORIS LEONIDOVICH. (1890–1960)
My Sister Life, 1922.
Themes and Variations, 1923.
Doctor Zhivago, 1958.

1923 Soviet Union-Moscow: The two early books of poems, highly considered abroad, caused the author to be denounced in the Soviet Union as a "decadent formalist." Consequently he turned to translating Shakespeare and other poets to earn a living.

1958 Soviet Union-Moscow: Pasternak submitted his novel, *Doctor Zhivago,* to the State Publishing House and sent a copy to a publisher in Italy. Moscow condemned the book and did not publish it. The author was compelled to ask the Italians to return the manuscript for "revisions," which they refused to do. The novel became a best seller in Europe and the United States and resulted in the author being awarded the Nobel prize for literature. The Soviet Union denounced the award with a scathing attack on the Swedish judges for a "hostile political act for recognizing a work withheld from Russian readers which was counterrevolutionary and slanderous." Pasternak was formally read out of the Soviet Union of Authors, deprived of his title of "Soviet writer," and forced to refuse the award, saying "in view of the meaning given to this honor in the community in which I belong, I should abstain from the undeserved prize that has been awarded to me."

1958 United States-New Haven: Yale University students and faculty signed a petition written by President A. Whitney Griswold protesting the vilification of Pasternak and urging that he go to Stockholm to receive the Nobel Prize and to welcome him back to continue his distinguished writing.

1961 A year after the death of Pasternak his friend and collaborator Olga Ivinskaya was arrested for allegedly receiving foreign royalties for Pasternak's works. She was sentenced to eight years imprisonment and hard labor in Siberia, and her daughter received three years for alleged complicity.

MARKS, PERCY. (1891–1956)
The Plastic Age, 1924.

1927 United States-Boston: Banned for revealing casual standards of college life.

MILLER, HENRY. (1891–)
Tropic of Cancer, 1934.
Tropic of Capricorn, 1938.
Sexus, 1949.

1934 United States: *Tropic of Cancer* banned by U.S. Customs.

1946 France-Paris: A prosecution of Henry Miller was undertaken, but owing to almost unanimous support for Miller from literary figures, the case was dropped.

1950 France: *Sexus* banned.

1953 United States-San Francisco: United States Court of Appeals upholds ban on the two *Tropics.*

1956 Norway: *Sexus* banned.

1961 United States: Grove Press published *Tropic of Cancer,* touching off a national controversy which led to many court decisions against the book, notably in New York, Florida, California and Massachusetts.

1964 United States: The United States Supreme Court found
Tropic of Cancer not obscene.

TOWSLEY, LENA. (1891–)
Peggy and Peter, What They Did Today, 1931.

1931 United States-New York: The first edition of this photo-
story book was printed without a picture of the children
saying their prayers at bedtime, as a quasi-intellectual parent
did not want the trouble of explaining the picture to her
children, who had never heard of God or religion. In later
editions the questionable picture was tipped in.

1930 Soviet Union: The Soviet Government, feeling somewhat the
same way about the religious question, acted similarly. Before the opening of the school season one million copies of a
new primary textbook were ready for release. Suddenly a
horrified official discovered that in a poem by Nekrasov
the word God (Bog) was spelled with a capital letter. To
reduce Bog to bog involved changing sixteen pages in each
of the million copies; but the change was made, regardless
of expense, and the books reached the Soviet children un-
contaminated.

ALDINGTON, RICHARD. (1892–1962)
Death of a Hero, 1929.

1929 England: In his preface, Aldington complained that he had
reluctantly deleted certain words and passages because his
publisher feared prosecution.

HUXLEY, ALDOUS. (1894–1963)
Antic Hay, 1923.
Point Counter Point, 1928.
Brave New World, 1932.
Eyeless in Gaza, 1936.

1930 United States-Boston: *Antic Hay* banned on grounds of
obscenity.
Ireland: *Point Counter Point* banned on the ground of
"offending public morals."

1932 Ireland: *Brave New World* banned.

1936 Ireland: *Eyeless in Gaza* banned.

1953 United States: *Antic Hay* was placed on the list of publications disapproved by the National Organization of Decent Literature.
Ireland: *Eyeless in Gaza* unbanned by Appeal Board. *Point Counter Point* and other books still banned.

KINSEY, ALFRED. (1894–1956)
Sexual Behavior in the Human Male, 1948.
Sexual Behavior in the Human Female, 1953.

1953 West Germany: Both books banned in United States Army post exchanges in Europe as having "no worthwhile interest for soldiers." Not stocked in Army libraries.
South Africa: Banned upon publication by the Interior Minister.
Ireland: Banned.

1954 Soviet Union-Moscow: *Sexual Behavior in the Human Female* reviewed eight months after publication and called "the cheapest pornographic hash clumsily masked as science."

1956 United States: Kinsey's collection of books, pictures, etc., imported from Europe and the Orient for the Institute for Sex Research Inc., brought to trial in Federal Court in New York after being held for six years by the U.S. Customs. The New York *Times* reported Dr. Kinsey as saying: "This is a real test of the right of scholars to have access to their material. . . . They have taken the position that the same prohibitions apply to us as would to a commercial enterprise. . ."

1957 The right to import was upheld and Kinsey's collection formed a nucleus of suppressed works at the University of Indiana, many of which were later issued along with scholarly analyses of them, *e.g., My Secret Life,* one of the most notorious examples of Victorian English pornography.

GRAVES, ROBERT. (1895–)
I, Claudius, 1934.

1955 South Africa: Banned under the Customs Act of 1955. The Board of Censors still maintains a list of over 4,000 prohibited titles, including Tennessee Williams' *Streetcar Named Desire* and D. H. Lawrence's *Aaron's Rod*.

WILSON, EDMUND. (1895–)
Memoirs of Hecate County, 1946.

1946 United States-New York: 130 copies were confiscated by the police from four Doubleday bookshops after the New York Society for the Suppression of Vice charged that it was salacious and lascivious. Fifty thousand copies had been sold in the four months since publication. The Court of Special Sessions adjudged the book obscene in a 2–1 decision and the publisher was fined $1,000. The District Attorney warned that anyone who sold a copy could be sentenced to a year's imprisonment.
Los Angeles: Booksellers were fined for sale of the book. The conviction was later upset upon appeal.
San Francisco: A bookseller was acquitted on a second trial, after the first trial resulted in a hung jury.
Philadelphia: Copies confiscated by police.
Massachusetts: Publishers ceased shipment to the state because of its censorship law.
1947 New York: Decision affirmed in the State Supreme Court's Appellate Division and later upheld by the State Court of Appeals.
1948 Washington: The first United States Supreme Court test of a state "obscene literature" statute, as applied to a book, resulted in a 4–4 split decision, allowing the conviction to stand.

FAULKNER, WILLIAM. (1897–1962)
Soldier's Pay, 1926.
Mosquitoes, 1927.
Sanctuary, 1931.
Pylon, 1935.
The Wild Palms, 1939.
The Hamlet, 1940.

1948 United States-Philadelphia: After a complaint from a fundamentalist minister that obscene books were being sold, the Chief Inspector of the Vice Squad assigned a patrolman to investigate. He bought about twenty-five books and marked the so-called improper words and passages—thus becoming the judge of what the people of Philadelphia should read. A raid without warrant followed on fifty-four bookshops and approximately 2,000 allegedly obscene books were seized, including *Mosquitoes, Sanctuary* and *The Wild Palms*. While action was pending, the police obtained warrants for the arrest of five booksellers and indictments against nine books. Also included in this case were such books as James T. Farrell's *Studs Lonigan* and *A World I Never Made*. The defense of these books was vigorously undertaken by their publishers.

1949 Judge Curtis Bok dismissed the indictments against the booksellers and said that the books "were an obvious effort to show life as it was."

1950 Sweden-Stockholm: Faulkner was awarded the Nobel prize for literature.

1950 The Superior Court of Pennsylvania upon appeal by the Commonwealth upheld the judgment of Judge Bok.

1954 *Sanctuary, Pylon* and *Soldier's Pay* were on the disapproved list of the National Organization of Decent Literature, and were also condemned by many local censorship groups throughout the country.

Ireland: Most of the author's writings were banned.

SMITH, LILLIAN. (1897–1966)
Strange Fruit, 1944.

1944 United States-Boston: *Strange Fruit* was forbidden to be sold in bookshops by the Board of Retail Book Merchants and the Commissioner of Police. Boston's behind-the-counter censorship of books was defied for the first time in sixty-six years by the Civil Liberties Union of Massachusetts. The case was forced into the courts through the purchase of the novel by Bernard De Voto from a Cambridge bookseller. In court the book was ruled obscene, indecent and impure because of its language. The bookseller was fined $200, but this was later reduced to $25. New York: The publisher was informed that the U.S. Post

Office Department had seized six copies of *Strange Fruit*
and would not receive any more copies for mailing, although 200,000 copies had been sold.

Detroit: As in Boston, the majority of bookstores entered
into a "gentlemen's agreement" with the Police Department
and removed the book from sale. However, the United
Automobile Workers' Book Shop refused to withdraw the
title as long as it could be obtained from the Public Library,
and appealed to its parent union, which prepared to defend
them legally if necessary. The Public Library insisted upon
keeping the book in circulation and the police ended the
controversy by lifting the ban.

1945 Boston: The Superior Court of Massachusetts on an appeal
from the Supreme Court upheld the 1944 conviction and
declared the novel a menace to the morals of youth.

1953 Ireland: Banned.

HEMINGWAY, ERNEST. (1898–1961)
The Sun Also Rises, 1926.
A Farewell to Arms, 1929.
To Have and Have Not, 1937.
For Whom the Bell Tolls, 1940.
Across the River and into the Trees, 1950.
The Old Man and the Sea, 1952.

1929 Italy: *A Farewell to Arms* was banned because of its pain-
fully accurate account of the Italian retreat from Caporetto.
United States: The screen version was privately censored
through Italian influence.
Boston: Five issues of *Scribner's Magazine* were prohibited
because they contained the story.

1929 Robert Herrick attacked *A Farewell to Arms* in an article
entitled "What Is Dirt?" in the November issue of *Bookman.*

1930 Boston: *The Sun Also Rises* was banned.

1933 Germany: Works burned in the Nazi bonfires.

1938 United States-Detroit: *To Have and Have Not* was removed
from public sale and from circulation in the public library,
but preserved among works by "writers of standing." It was

also barred from sale by the Prosecutor of Wayne County on complaint of Catholic organizations. The novel was reported by the American Civil Liberties Union as the only book suppressed during the year.
New York: Distribution forbidden in the Borough of Queens.

1939 Ireland: *A Farewell to Arms* banned.

1941 United States-New York: When the Pulitzer Prize Advisory Board recommended *For Whom the Bell Tolls* for the 1940 prize, Columbia University President Nicholas Murray Butler said, "I hope that you will reconsider before you ask the University to be associated with an award for a work of this nature." There was no Pulitzer Prize for fiction for 1940. The Post Office in the same year declared the book nonmailable.

1953 *The Sun Also Rises* and *Across the River and into the Trees* were banned in Ireland.

1954 Sweden-Stockholm: Awarded Nobel prize for literature for *The Old Man and the Sea.*

1956 South Africa-Johannesburg: *Across the River and into the Trees* was banned as "objectionable and obscene."

1960 United States-California: *The Sun Also Rises* banned from San Jose schools. All of Hemingway's books withdrawn from Riverside school libraries.

1962 "Texans for America" opposed textbooks which referred students to books by Hemingway.

WAUGH, ALEC. (1898–)
The Loom of Youth, 1917.

1917 England: Waugh, in his autobiography, says "In many schools the book was banned and boys were caned for reading it." Despite this attack the book has never been out of print.

REMARQUE, ERICH MARIA. (1898–)
All Quiet on the Western Front, 1929.
The Road Back, 1931.
Three Comrades, 1937.
Flotsam, 1941.

1929 United States-Boston: *All Quiet on the Western Front* was banned on grounds of obscenity, although it was expurgated at the suggestion of the Book-of-the-Month Club, whose selection it was.

Chicago: Copies of the English translation were seized by U.S. Customs.

Austria: Soldiers were forbidden to read the book.

Czechoslovakia: Barred from the military libraries by the war department.

1930 Germany-Thuringia: Banned.

1933 Italy: The Italian translation was banned because of the book's anti-war propaganda.

Germany: All works consigned to the Nazi bonfires.

1953 Ireland: *The Road Back, Flotsam* and *Three Comrades* were still banned.

NABOKOV, VLADIMIR. (1899–)
Lolita, 1955.

1955 Nabokov completed *Lolita* in 1954, but could not find a publisher. Olympia Press issued it and it was held admissible by U.S. Customs, but not by the British. Graham Greene's praise of it set off a long controversy.

1956 France-Paris: Banned as obscene. U.S. Customs pronounced the book unobjectionable. *Lolita* thus could not be legally exported from France, but smuggled copies could be legally imported into the United States.

United States: Publishers thought the book unworthy of publication, but it came out abridged in a magazine, *Anchor Review 2*.

1958 The book was finally published by Putnam.

1959 England: Freely published.

France: Ban lifted.

Argentina-Buenos Aires: The court said *Lolita* was not

banned because of crude passages, but because the whole
work reflected moral disintegration and reviled humanity.
The ban was again upheld in 1962.

1960 New Zealand: Banned by the Supreme Court.

DISNEY, WALT. (1901–1966)
Mickey Mouse, an internationally syndicated comic
strip.

1932 United States: A *Mickey Mouse* cartoon was suppressed because it showed a cow resting in a pasture reading Elinor
Glyn's *Three Weeks.*

1937 Yugoslavia-Belgrade: *The Mickey Mouse Comic Strip* was
banned because of a supposedly anti-monarchical story
picturing a plot against a young king and a conspiracy to
place an impostor on the throne. Concurrently a regency
headed by Prince Paul was ruling the country during the
minority of King Peter.

1938 Italy-Rome: The National Conference of Juvenile Literature decided that *Mickey Mouse* was unsuitable for the
minds of children, and editors were instructed to eliminate
it as contrary to "Italian inspiration as to racism, and
exaltation of the imperial, Fascist and Mussolinian tone in
which we live." Children, they said, should be trained in the
principles of "sleeping with the head on a knapsack." However, a distinction was made between guns handled by organized youth and gunplay as depicted in the comics.

1954 Germany-East Berlin: Communists raided the schools in
search of Western books. They found *Mickey Mouse* comics and banned them because *Mickey* was classed as an anti-
Red rebel.

GUTHRIE, ALFRED BERTRAM, JR. (1901–)
The Big Sky, 1947.
The Way West, 1949.

1962 United States-Texas: Banned in Amarillo, along with many
other novels.

HANLEY, JAMES. (1901–)
Boy, 1931.

1931 England: The second and third editions were progressively bowdlerized by the publisher. A reprint of the third edition was seized at a circulating library in Manchester. The book was later defended eloquently by E. M. Forster at a meeting of the International Congress of Authors in Paris.

STEINBECK, JOHN. (1902–1968)
The Grapes of Wrath, 1939.
The Wayward Bus, 1947.

1939 United States-St. Louis: Seven months after publication of *The Grapes of Wrath,* three copies were ordered burned by the public library because of the vulgar words employed by the characters. After a protest by the National Council on Freedom From Censorship, the book was placed on a shelf for "adults only."

Kansas City: Banned here and in towns in Oklahoma.

New York: The book was assigned reading in sociology classes at the College of the City of New York. At this time, there were 360,000 copies in print.

California: The Associated Farmers of Kern County, whose policies had been attacked, mapped a statewide ban in schools and libraries against the book as being derogatory to the state.

1942–1943 Germany: By order of the Propaganda Administration, *The Grapes of Wrath* was issued in a German translation.

1953 United States: *The Wayward Bus,* although a Pulitzer Prize winner, was placed on the list of books disapproved by the Gathings Committee and by censorship groups in many cities.

Ireland: Works banned.

CALDWELL, ERSKINE. (1903–)
Tobacco Road, 1932.
God's Little Acre, 1933.

1933 United States-New York: *God's Little Acre,* taken to court on charges of obscenity by the New York Society for the Prevention of Vice, was exonerated. The decision handed down by City Magistrate Benjamin Greenspan marked a milepost in the fight against censorship. It rested on the fact that the book must be considered in its entirety, not in isolated passages; that a cross-section of representative people were relevant to the case; that the book was honest and sincere in its intent, and obviously "not a work of pornography"; that it "has no tendency to incite its readers to behave like its characters"; and that its use of coarse and vulgar language was not censurable, since "the court may not require the author to put refined language in the mouths of primitive people."

1935 Chicago: The play *Tobacco Road* was banned as indecent and forbidden in many other cities as well, including Detroit, St. Paul, Minneapolis, Utica and Tulsa. In Washington, D.C., Representative Deen of Georgia made an impassioned appeal to Congress to stop the showing of "the infamous, wicked, untruth (sic) portrait" of his district as portrayed in *Tobacco Road.* However, a posse of six assistant district attorneys was dispatched to the theatre to see for themselves and they returned a verdict favorable to the play.

1946 St. Paul: *God's Little Acre* was banned but was readily available across the Mississippi in Minneapolis.

1947 Denver: The novel was banned in the twenty-five-cent edition to keep the book out of the hands of teen-age children.

1948 Philadelphia: Seized in the mass bookstore raid by the police, and later exonerated.
Ireland: Banned.

1950 Boston: Banned from the state as indecent, obscene and impure by the full bench of the Massachusetts Supreme Court. The world's best selling modern novel, more than

6,500,000 copies of the twenty-five-cent edition alone were sold.

1953 Chicago: *God's Little Acre* was listed as disapproved by the National Organization of Decent Literature.

England: The novel was included in the *National Newsagent Bookseller Stationer* list of nearly 700 books named for destruction by local magistrates. Also included was *Studs Lonigan* by James T. Farrell (*q.v.*).

United States: Blacklisted by the Gathings Committee.

Ireland: *God's Little Acre* and *Tobacco Road* banned.

1960 Australia: *God's Little Acre* found obscene and banned by the Supreme Court.

CONNELL, VIVIAN. (1903–)
The Chinese Room, 1942.
September in Quinze, 1952.

1953 United States-New Jersey: Matthew F. Melko, prosecuting attorney of Middlesex County, sent to wholesalers a list of objectionable titles compiled by a so-called citizens' committee, suggesting that such books be withdrawn. The publishers of *The Chinese Room,* Bantam Books, represented by Horace S. Manges, brought suit. Judge Sidney Goldman of the Superior Court ruled that the prosecutor violated the constitutional guarantee of freedom of the press and held that the book in question was unobjectionable.

1954 The New Jersey Supreme Court sustained this ruling, but limited itself to the single title in litigation. It deleted certain broader principles of the lower court's judgment involving the prosecutor's right to promulgate lists, enlist aid from unofficial committees, and threaten sellers. A rehearing was denied.

Great Britain-London: By jury trial, *September in Quinze* was judged an obscene libel, and its publishers were fined $4200. This verdict followed the so-called Secker case in which Justice Stable acquitted the publishers of *The Philanderer* by Stanley Kauffmann (*q.v.*) with his widely praised reversal of the traditional Cockburn decision.

KANTOR, MACKINLAY. (1904–)
Andersonville, 1955.

1956 United States-New York: Awarded Pulitzer Prize.

1962 Texas: Widely attacked in the United States, it was successfully banned in Amarillo.

FARRELL, JAMES T. (1904–)
Studs Lonigan: A Trilogy, 1932–35.
A World I Never Made, 1936.

1936 United States-New York: Advertising for *A World I Never Made* was refused by the New York *Times* on publication.

1937 New York: The novel was the only book prosecuted by the New York Society for the Suppression of Vice during the year, although it was written on a Guggenheim Fellowship. In court, where many prominent writers testified favorably, Magistrate Henry H. Curran exonerated *A World I Never Made* and ruled that "a whole novel should not be condemned because of objection to parts as obscene, lewd and lascivious."

Milwaukee: The novel was seized by the Chief of Police as vulgar, obscene and unfit for children. The author appealed to the Socialist Mayor and to the Socialist Chief of Police "as a Socialist comrade to do all in your power to halt this illegal action on the part of the police."

New York: Farrell was awarded a $2,500 Book-of-the-Month-Club Fellowship. The award was made "to the man rather than to a particular book."

1942 England-London: The trilogy *Studs Lonigan* was dropped from the American Library Association list of books interpreting the United States. Consequently Constable & Co., publishers, were refused a permit to import American sheets. This amounted to a virtual ban in England as they had insufficient paper to publish it there. However when paper was secured 5,000 copies were printed.

Germany: The sending of *Studs Lonigan* to prisoners of war was banned.

Canada: *Studs Lonigan* was refused entry as being of an indecent and immoral character.

1953 United States: *Studs Lonigan* and *A World I Never Made* were on the blacklists of the Gathings Committee and the National Organization of Decent Literature.
Minnesota-St. Cloud: Works banned.
Ireland: Works banned.

1957 Works were banned in overseas libraries controlled by the United States Information Agency.

DELMAR, VIÑA. (1905–)
Bad Girl, 1928.

1928 United States-Boston: Banned by the Watch and Ward Society, although it was a selection of the Literary Guild of America.

1933 Ireland: Prohibited for describing an illegal abortion too graphically.

O'HARA, JOHN. (1905–1970)
Appointment in Samarra, 1934.
Ten North Frederick, 1956.

1941 United States: *Appointment in Samarra* declared nonmailable by the Post Office Department, although it was freely sold.

1957 A series of local bans and seizures spread over a two-year period during the height of *Ten North Frederick*'s popularity. Cleveland, Albany, and Omaha were involved.
Detroit: This book, which won the 1956 National Book Award for fiction, was banned in the paper edition by Police Commissioner Piggins, acting under the Michigan obscenity statute. Although the bound edition had been sold in Detroit bookstores for a year and was available in the Public Library it also fell under the ban. A Federal District Court ruled against the Detroit Police Commissioner.

1958 New York: The Albany County Supreme Court indicted Bantam Books, John O'Hara, and the distributors of *Ten North Frederick* for conspiring to publish and distribute an obscene book. The defendants examined the testimony and found that only certain passages had been read. This appears to be the first time following the Roth decision that the validity of an indictment involving a charge of obscenity has been challenged in any jurisdiction on the ground that the entire publication had not been read to or by the grand jury. The ban was lifted.

SARTRE, JEAN-PAUL. (1905–)

1948 Italy-Rome: Works listed in the *Index*.

1954 Works removed from United States Information Agency libraries throughout the world.

GENET, JEAN. (1910–)
Our Lady of the Flowers, 1942.

1957 England: A two-volume edition of Genet's novels, in French, ordered by the Birmingham Public Library, was seized.

1964 According to a letter by Genet's publisher, Maurice Giro-dias, to *Newsweek,* the English translation was banned in France "five or six years ago" but the original French text was available.

DURRELL, LAWRENCE. (1912–)
The Black Book, 1938.

1961 United States: Seized by the Customs Bureau. Subsequently successfully published in the United States.

SHULMAN, IRVING. (1913–)
The Amboy Dukes, 1947.

1949 Canada-Brantford, Ontario: Cleared of obscenity charges by Judge D. J. Cowan.

1949–50 United States: Book under fire by local authorities in Milwaukee, Detroit, Newark and elsewhere.

1954 On disapproved list of National Organization of Decent Literature.

BURROUGHS, WILLIAM. (1914–)
Naked Lunch, 1959.

1965 United States-Boston: Found obscene in Superior Court. The finding was reversed by the State Supreme Court the following year. Burroughs' book was one of many that came under widespread attack in the 1960s.

FAST, HOWARD. (1914–)
Citizen Tom Paine, 1943.

1947 United States-New York: Banned from the high school libraries in a vote of 6–1 by the Board of Education because it was allegedly written by a spokesman of a totalitarian movement and because it contained incidents and expressions not desirable for children, and was improper and indecent.

Almost a million copies of the book had been sold. It had been distributed to the armed forces abroad and to citizens of liberated countries.

The ban was strongly opposed at a public meeting by Marc Connelly, head of the Censorship Committee of the Authors League of America, and by other organizations. Connelly demanded that "the bigotry behind its condemnation be investigated in the interest of public welfare." The ban was supported by Rupert Hughes, president of the American Writers Association, who said the Board must not "yield to a propaganda drive."

1953 Soviet Union-Moscow: The Stalin Peace Prize was awarded to Howard Fast for "strengthening peace between peoples." The prize was established in 1950 in honor of Stalin's seventieth birthday and is said to be worth $25,000.

1953 The book was withdrawn from United States Information Agency libraries overseas.

1957 United States: Following the Soviet invasion of Hungary, Fast renounced his loyalty to Communism, despite the enormous popularity of his works in the Soviet Union and the honors bestowed upon him by the Soviet government.

WILLIAMS, TENNESSEE. (1914–)

1965 Portugal: All writings banned.

DAVIE, EMILY. (1915–)
Profile of America, 1954.

1954 The United States Information Agency sent 30,000 copies overseas.

1955 A House of Representatives Subcommittee on Appropriations specified that no funds were to be used for any re-orders of *Profile of America*. Subcommittee Chairman Rooney called it a "fine book for American consumption. But when it comes to showing foreigners what foul balls we are, that is something different." Objections were based on a photograph of an eighteenth-century school, a quotation from Thoreau, and an excerpt from *Ah, Wilderness!* alleged to be obscene. Despite Senate approval, the funds were not granted for re-order.

MILLER, ARTHUR. (1915–)
A View From the Bridge, 1955.

1956 England-London: The Lord Chamberlain refused a license for performance of the play, which had won both the New York Drama Critics Circle Award and the Pulitzer Prize.

KAUFFMANN, STANLEY. (1916–)
The Philanderer, 1953.

1954 England-London: The novel, originally published in America under the title of *The Tightrope* (1952), was involved in the British courts in a nominal damage verdict brought against a lending library on the Isle of Man. In London the Director of Public Prosecutions charged that the book was "obscene in the sense that it tends to corrupt and deprave the minds of those into whose hands it might fall, not only in certain passages but in the whole tendency of the book." This charge was worded to comply with the traditional test of obscenity under British law, Justice Cockburn's decision in 1868 in *Regina* v. *Hicklin*.

Justice Stable, in his charge to the jury, emphasized that the 1868 test had to be applied in the light of modern standards. He pointed out that while there were two schools of thought on the subject of sex which were "poles apart," the stand taken by average, decent people was somewhere in between.

The jury was given three days in which to read the book and charged that their verdict would have great bearing on where the line was to be drawn between liberty and license. The publishers were found not guilty and Justice Stable's decision was heralded as a fresh reappraisal of the 1868 decision.

SALINGER, J. D. (1919–)
The Catcher in the Rye, 1951.

1955 United States: Beginning this year and extending to the present, this book has been a favorite target of censors. Literally hundreds of attempts have been made to ban the book in schools throughout the United States, many of them successful. As recently as 1968, a group in Minnesota attacked a high school administration for permitting it in the library.

1957 Australia: Despite a presentation gift by the U.S. Ambassador, Australian Customs seized a shipment of this book.

THE LITTLE REVIEW

1917 United States-New York: An issue of this famous periodical was confiscated by postal authorities, whose action was later upheld by a Federal Court. The occasion was the publication of a story by Wyndham Lewis which reflected adversely on war.

1921 New York: Margaret Anderson, the editor of *The Little Review,* having been arrested the previous summer for printing "obscene" excerpts from Joyce's *Ulysses* (*q.v.*), was found guilty and fined $50. The New York *Times,* commenting on the case, observed that *Ulysses* was a trivial work, not worth the trouble of prosecuting.

WINSOR, KATHLEEN. (1919–)
Forever Amber, 1944.

1946 United States: Springfield, Mass. A temporary injunction was issued against sale of the book, the first to come under the new Massachusetts censorship law of 1945, which although it did not change the definition of obscenity, set up a new procedure in the case of books sold to persons eighteen years of age or older, whereby the action was to be against the book, not the distributor, and must be instigated by the district attorney or attorney general.

1946 England: Copies burned at British ports and by the public library in Birmingham.

1947 Boston: The book was acquitted in Suffolk County Superior Court. On appeal, the decision was upheld in 1948 by the Massachusetts Supreme Court. Judge Frank J. Donahue found the novel to be "obscene, indecent or impure," but he added that it was "a soporific rather than an aphrodisiac . . . that while the novel was conducive to sleep, it was not conducive to a desire to sleep with a member of the opposite sex."

This was the first instance of a book being cleared by the high court of Massachusetts, four others having been condemned since the turn of the century. These were Elinor Glyn's *Three Weeks,* Dreiser's *An American Tragedy,* Lawrence's *Lady Chatterley's Lover* and Lillian Smith's *Strange Fruit.*

1953 Ireland: Banned.

GRIFFIN, JOHN HOWARD. (1920–)
The Devil Rides Outside, 1952.
Black Like Me, 1961.

1954 United States-Detroit: *The Devil Rides Outside* was one of 192 books classified as "objectionable" by the city prosecutor's office, 46 others having been previously classified as "partly objectionable" under the Detroit system of police censorship established in 1951.

The district sales manager of Pocket Books, publisher of

the paperbound reprint edition, was charged with the sale of an obscene book, found guilty and fined.

1957 In a notable decision, *Butler* v. *Michigan,* the Supreme Court reversed the conviction. Justice Frankfurter said that the statute under which the conviction was obtained would "reduce the adult population of Michigan to reading what was fit for children." This case made a conclusive breakthrough in eliminating the Hicklin rule, which had been the legal guide in obscenity cases for a century.

1966 The paperback edition of *Black Like Me* was widely attacked as unfit for children. In Wisconsin, a man sued his local school board for damage to his child; the case was dismissed.

JONES, JAMES. (1921–)
From Here to Eternity, 1951.

1951 United States: This book was unofficially censored in Holyoke and Springfield, Massachusetts and in Denver, Colorado.

1953 New Jersey-Jersey City: Police "suggested" to dealers that they remove the title from newsstands and book outlets. Most dealers complied, but after it had been pointed out by a representative of the American Book Publishers Council that this was contrary to a New Jersey court decision, the book was again placed on sale.

1954 United States: On disapproved list of the National Organization of Decent Literature.

1955 Declared nonmailable by the Post Office, although it was a best seller for four years.

BISHOP, LEONARD. (1922–)
Down All Your Streets, 1952.

1953 United States-Youngstown, Ohio: The Chief of Police of this city had ordered some 335 paperbound books removed from newsstands as allegedly obscene. Suit was brought by the New American Library, publisher of *Down All Your Streets* and some of the other books so banned, with Roosevelt, Freidin and Littauer serving as attorneys. Federal

Judge Charles J. McNamee, of the U.S. District Court in Cleveland, enjoined the police officer from such action, pointing out that he "was without authority to censor books."

1954 The city of Youngstown brought suit against a local distributor of paperbound books on the charge of distributing for sale a book of "obscene and immoral nature." Municipal Judge Forrest J. Cavalier dismissed the charges, agreeing with the defense that the word "immoral" in the original affidavit was too vague.

WILLINGHAM, CALDER. (1922–)
End as a Man, 1947.

1947 United States-New York: John S. Sumner of the New York Society for the Suppression of Vice sought a ban on this frank portrayal of life in a South Carolina military college. However, charges were dismissed by Magistrate Frederick L. Strong in New York's Municipal Term Court a few weeks later.

1948 Philadelphia: *End as a Man* was among other titles seized in the Philadelphia raids. Judge Curtis Bok in the Court of Quarter Sessions acquitted the whole list. (*See* Faulkner.)

1950 Pennsylvania: This decision was appealed to the Pennsylvania Superior Court, but it was upheld.

MAILER, NORMAN. (1923–)
The Naked and the Dead, 1948.

1949 England: This book created quite a stir when publication was first announced. But on May 23, according to the New York *Times,* Attorney General Sir Hartley Shawcross told the House of Commons that no action would be taken against the distribution of the book.

Canada: Rinehart, the American publisher, was informed by the Canadian Customs that the book "cannot be permitted entry into Canada."

Australia: Banned.

1954 United States-Georgia: The State Literature Commission investigated this novel, together with several joke books and magazines.

BALDWIN, JAMES. (1924–)
Another Country, 1962.

1963 United States-New Orleans: Considered obscene, the book was banned from the public library. After a year of litigation, it was restored.
Australia: Banned.

1964 New Zealand: The Indecent Publications Tribunal found *Another Country* not obscene.

1965 Chicago: A parent protested his daughter's reading the book at Wright Junior College.

METALIOUS, GRACE. (1924?–1964)
Peyton Place, 1956.

1958 Canada: Temporary ban lifted.

1960 United States-New York: Accepted by New York public libraries.

DONLEAVY, JAMES PATRICK. (1926–)
The Ginger Man, 1955.

1955 England: Originally published by Girodias in Paris, Donleavy expurgated his own text to permit publication in England.

REGISTER OF PROHIBITED PUBLICATIONS

1929 Ireland: A Censorship of Publications Board was established and empowered to report to the Minister of Justice on books dealing with obscenity, contraception, and abortion. The Minister is in turn to issue prohibition orders without legal challenge. The *Register of Prohibited Publications* at present contains about 4000 titles. In effect it resembles the *Index Librorum Prohibitorum.*

Appendix

TRENDS IN CENSORSHIP

THE POLITICAL AND RELIGIOUS CONTROL OF BOOKS

In the history of censorship, the oldest and most frequently recurring controls have been those designed to prevent unorthodox and unpopular expressions of political or religious opinions. A notable example of the latter was the Roman Catholic *Index Librorum Prohibitorum* which, at the time it was abrogated, restrained the reading of nearly a sixth of the world's population. The Church's regulation of books can be traced back to Apostolic times, when the Ephesian converts of St. Paul made a bonfire of hundreds of volumes catering to superstition. Most of the early lists and decrees, however, were concerned with establishing which books were to be accepted as part of the Bible, which were recommended reading and which were heretical. In 1515 the Lateran Council established the principle of ecclesiastical licensing, a procedure which was formalized and given potency by the Council of Trent in 1546, with the forbidding of the sale or possession of anonymous religious books. It was Pope Paul IV who authorized the first list of banned books in 1557. For nearly four hundred years, the list was issued in numerous editions, with occasional additions and deletions. The last edition was published in 1948, with a list of more than 4,000 titles, including some of the masterworks of the Western world. Publication of the *Index* ceased in 1966. Without rescinding the previous decisions, the Church's action effectively ended official censorship and control over what Roman Catholics might be permitted to read.

In this century, political censorship has consistently taken more dramatic forms and received far greater notoriety than religious bannings. However, recent episodes of suppression, although numerous, are quite limited in scope when compared to the era of Nazi Germany and the Communist purge which followed. The first large-scale demonstration occurred on May 10, 1933, when students gathered 25,000 volumes by Jewish authors and burned them in the square in front of the University of Berlin. The bonfire was watched by 40,000 unenthusiastic people in a drizzling rain. Joseph Goebbels, the Minister of Public Enlightenment, delivered an address on "the symbolic significance of the gesture." Similar demonstrations were held at many other German universities. In Munich 5,000 school children, who had formerly seen Marxist literature publicly burned, were enjoined: "as you watch the fire burn these un-German books, let it also burn into your hearts love of the Fatherland." Students entered the bookstores and took without remuneration the books they considered eligible for the bonfire, and had to be prevented from confiscating books from the University Library.

The following list consists of some of the most important authors whose works were sacrificed at the fires.

Sholom Asch, Lion Feuchtwanger, Maxim Gorky, Stefan Zweig, Karl Marx, Sigmund Freud, Helen Keller, Jack London, Ernest Hemingway, John Dos Passos, Jakob Wasserman, Emil Ludwig, Arthur Schnitzler, Leon Trotsky, V. I. Lenin, Josef Stalin, Grigori S. Zinoviev, Alfred Adler, Gotthold Lessing, Franz Werfel, Hugo Munsterberg, Thomas Mann, Heinrich Mann, Erich Maria Remarque, Albert Einstein, Heinrich Heine, Felix Mendelssohn, Maximilian Harden, Kurt Eisner, Henri Barbusse, Rosa Luxemburg, Upton Sinclair, Judge Ben Lindsay, Arnold Zweig.

This great destruction of books by the Nazis continued until World War II. In 1938 they made a cultural purge of Austria. Booksellers were forced to clear their shelves of proscribed works, and either to conceal or destroy them. When word of the purge reached the United States, many offers to buy the books were sent to Vienna by universities and individuals. Some eventually did reach this country.

In Salzburg 15,000 people watched a "purification bonfire" of one copy each of 2,000 volumes, including Jewish and Catholic books. The ceremony was started by a schoolboy who threw a copy of Schuschnigg's *Three Times Austria* on the gasoline-soaked pyre. Meanwhile the crowd sang "Deutschland Über Alles" in the gaily lighted square. The proceedings were under the auspices of the National Socialist (Nazi) Teachers' Association, which had appealed to the public to give up all "objectionable literature," and it was said that the destruction of 30,000 more volumes would follow.

In Leipzig many of the same books which were burned in the Nazi bonfire of 1933 were suppressed, and in Czechoslovakia the Education Ministry ordered all public libraries to remove and destroy all unpatriotic books, particularly by patriots including ex-President Beneš.

In 1944 the great "book city" of Leipzig suffered the loss of many valuable books by the Allied bombings, and in 1946 the Coordinating Council of the American Military Government in Germany ordered Nazi memorials to be destroyed. The object was to eliminate the "spirit of German militarism and Nazism as far as possible."

This order to cleanse the German mentality was issued just as the eleventh anniversary of the Nazi "Burning of the Books" was being observed by the free world, and it caused much sharp comment. Included were the works of Hitler, Goebbels, Mussolini and Karl Marx. The books were placed on the restricted lists in libraries, or in some instances pulped, but no burnings were known to have taken place. At the same time the Communists in East Germany were doing the same thing from their own point of view.

In 1953, in East Germany, the Communist cultural advisers removed from the libraries, schools and bookshops at least 5,000,000 volumes by German, Nazi and foreign authors. Even Marx and Engels did not escape and were expurgated or rewritten "with historically important additions." It is said that books written before the war about the "good old days" were especially feared.

In 1953–4 it was reported by the refugees from East Berlin that all printed matter including picture papers and crossword puzzles sent to East Germany were confiscated at the border. As recently as 1969, East German guards at Rudolphstein refused passage to West Berlin of copies of Konrad Adenauer's memoirs and of road maps showing Germany's boundaries before World War II.

No purpose would be served in detailing all the known specific instances of censorship in Communist nations. The right of the state to determine what shall or shall not be read is firmly established in Communist countries, and the catalog of banned or emasculated works is long. Soviet censorship is particularly fascinating because it appears to rise and fall in intensity in accordance with the currents of policy considerations as they affect the state. Notable literary figures in the Soviet Union have been embroiled from time to time, and efforts to restrain authors from expressing opinions contrary to party dictates are frequently matters of intense debate in the Soviet press.

The more spectacular censorship moves in the Soviet Union include the unsuccessful effort to prevent publication abroad of *Doctor Zhivago* by Boris Pasternak (*q.v.*). The degree of effort that the Soviet Union is willing to expend to suppress information is astonishing to Westerners. Following the death of Stalin, Lavrenti Beria, the head of the Soviet Secret Police, was discredited and later executed. *The Great Soviet Encyclopedia,* which had already been published and distributed abroad, contained a lengthy article on Beria. This article was ordered to be excised from all existing copies of that particular volume and sheets containing an article on The Bering Sea were substituted.

OVERSEAS LIBRARIES

In 1953 a great outcry went up over the alleged "book burnings" in the approximately 200 United States Information Agency libraries overseas. More than two million books stood on their shelves and they were visited by 36 million people a year. The purpose of these centers has been to provide a "balanced presentation" of American life and ideas through books and periodicals. Early in 1953 a Senate subcommittee, headed by Senator Joseph R. McCarthy, had been investigating the activities of the International Information Administration of the State Department. A series of confusing directives, which came from the State Department during that spring, led to different interpretations in libraries in the various capitals, the resulting book bannings causing serious damage to United States prestige abroad. During this time Senator McCarthy's staff men, Roy Cohn and David Schine, were making their quick survey of our overseas libraries. They visited seven European countries in eighteen days and turned in the spectacular report that there were 30,000 books by pro-Communist authors in the libraries. This later turned out to be a gross exaggeration.

It was said that more than forty authors were involved in the books withdrawn during this period. The debate over the selection of books for the overseas libraries culminated in July of that year with a directive from the State Department reaffirming the fundamental policy of selecting books which would reflect a representative picture of the United States. The books of eight known or avowed Communists were permanently banned and the books of some twenty other writers who had refused to testify as to their Communist affiliations before Senate investigating committees were banned "pending further examination."

Secretary of State John Foster Dulles testified that to his knowledge only eleven books had actually been burned by overzealous librarians, and that the other questionable books had been withdrawn from circulation for further consideration—a very small percentage of the two million books which have proved invaluable in the many countries where the libraries of the United States Information Agency have operated so efficiently and so successfully.

On June 14, 1953, President Eisenhower made his famous speech at Dartmouth College, "Don't join the book burners." The speech reasoned that Communism would be defeated only by our understanding of what it is and what it teaches. In order "to fight it with something better," we also should not attempt "to conceal the thinking of our own people . . . even if they think ideas that are contrary to ours." Excitement blazed anew and the press questioned the connection between the speech and the overseas library furore. The President, at a press conference, assured reporters that there was no connection between the two, that he was not familiar with the State Department directives to the libraries, but that he was against book burning and the suppression of ideas. However, to quote from the press conference record, the President's comments were that: "it is perfectly proper to bar certain books from the mails, as is done, and he would do it now"; that "he did not believe the standards of essential human dignity and decency ought to be violated," and that "Overseas, he saw no reason for bringing these (questionable) books out unless there was some area where we believed we had to show a particular group what Communism was, out of the mouths of the Communist leaders themselves. He added that he was not an apostle of the doctrine that all generalizations are always true."

Although the McCarthy episode has long passed, new accounts of library censorship overseas are not infrequent. The United States Information Agency banning of *The Ugly American* by William J. Lederer from its overseas libraries generated a great deal of unfavorable publicity in 1958. A year later the ban was lifted. In December 1969, a weekly news magazine reported that the USIA had barred the distribution of some two dozen books to one of its European libraries. The magazine went on to explain that six full-time reviewers screen books for the USIA into three categories: (1) recommended, to be "pushed hard" for overseas use (about 70 titles a month make the grade); (2) noncontroversial books that any USIA library can get by specifically requesting them from Washington; (3) books that raise questions about American policy and that the USIA believes might be "misunderstood" or "offensive" overseas.

Some of the banned books and the official USIA reasons for refusing them follow:

Henry Steele Commager's *Freedom and Order:* "The value of the rest of the book does not begin to overcome the liability of the 30-plus pages condemning American policies in Vietnam."

George R. Stewart's *Not So Rich As You Think:* "The book just wouldn't help to 'glamorize our program,' nor will it help other nations prevent or solve similar problems."

James Baldwin's *Tell Me How Long the Train's Been Gone:* "A quote from Mr. Baldwin to the effect that 'My countrymen impressed me simply as being, on the whole, the emptiest and most unattractive people in the world.' "

LIBRARY CENSORSHIP

Libraries in the United States felt the pressure of censorship long before the overseas libraries were subjected to such investigation. As early as 1941 Governor Eugene Talmadge of Georgia ordered removed from college and school libraries in his state books unfavorable to the South, the Bible, or the state of Georgia. He announced that he would ask the 1943 legislature to order the burning of library books advocating interracial cooperation. Although this particular censorship move did not materialize, that state is still the scene of censorship activities. In 1959 the Georgia Board of Education voted to require a stamp of approval from its literary committee on all library books after a board member warned that pro-integration literature was worming its way into the libraries. Two years later, the Georgia Library Association was forced to appeal to Chatham County grand jurors and to the president of the county board of education to protect their libraries from what it called "witch hunts." The action stemmed from the removal by the grand jury of four titles from Savannah high school libraries because they allegedly contained immoral material.

The librarian of Bartlesville, Oklahoma, was dismissed in 1950 after thirty-one years of service because she had participated in local group discussions on race relations and had certain magazines on the library shelves which a Citizens' Committee considered undesirable. Although the library had been administered by an autonomous board, which supported the librarian's position in all but one respect, the City Commission passed a new ordinance gaining control of the library and dismissing the old library board. The librarian and a member of the old board carried the case to the Oklahoma Supreme Court where, in 1952, the court ruled against them.

In the fall of 1952 the Boston Public Library was attacked by one of the city's newspapers, the Boston *Post,* for having Communist material, not on its open shelves, but in its reference collection. The Director of the library argued that all aspects of political, international and other questions must be available for the information of the citizens of the city. This established policy of the library was upheld by its board by a 3–2 vote.

Several other cities, notably San Antonio, Texas, and Dubuque, Iowa, faced similar censorship attacks on their public libraries in recent years. In Illinois some four hundred titles, involving between 6,000 and 8,000 volumes, were removed from circulation in the state libraries in December 1953, after the mother of a thirteen-year-old girl complained that she obtained a book which was "offensive." However, these were all reclassified "for adult consumption" early in 1954. The State Librarian originally ordered books "of a salacious, vulgar or obscene" character to be taken out of circulation, but later stated that his order "was never intended to result in what has been termed a wholesale withdrawal of books."

Similarly, in 1959, *The Rabbits' Wedding*, a book for children aged three to seven, was banished to the "reserved" shelf of the Alabama Public Library Service Division after the Alabama State Senate charged that the book represented a sneaky appeal for racial integration. In it, a black rabbit and a white rabbit get married at a moonlight ceremony in a forest. On the "reserved" shelf, *The Rabbits' Wedding* joined other books considered pro-integration and books considered obscene.

Obscenity was the charge leveled against *The Arrangement*, a novel by Elia Kazan, when it was barred from an Iowa municipal library in 1967. The publisher of the book, which at that time was on top of the nation's best seller list, countered this action by offering a free copy to every adult head of family in the community of 8,600 residents. This countermeasure called on the town citizens to decide for themselves if their library board was "practicing a form of censorship inconsistent with American tradition." After more than 800 free copies were requested, the publisher said: "If there is a good deal of discussion, pro and con, whether or not the book is obscene, we will have reached our objective. The point is that a library board should not make any book unavailable to the members of a community."

For some time a slang dictionary was the object of controversy in California. Agitation against *A Dictionary of American Slang* began in 1963 when Max Rafferty, Superintendent of Public Instruction, suggested that a "little bit of censorship" was necessary to remove the book from school libraries. To document their case that the book was "dirty," supporters of Mr. Rafferty combed through the dictionary's 8,000-odd entries, found the 150 dirtiest and listed them in a mimeographed publication. Although the book was banned in several communities and literally burned in at least one other, most libraries decided to keep the book for restricted use by serious students.

This use of reserved or restricted shelves has been one of several ways in which librarians have attempted to beat censors at their own game. The Fiske Report, *Book Selection and Censorship: A Study of School and Public Libraries in California,* published in 1959, clearly established a do-it-yourself movement among librarians. Of the ninety libraries and 204 librarians sampled in twenty-six localities, two thirds of the respondents reported refusals to purchase because of the controversial nature of a book or its author, one third reported the permanent removal or restriction of controversial materials, and a fifth reported an habitual avoidance of all controversial matter.

PAPERBOUND BOOKS

In the early 1950's approximately 1,000 paperbound titles were being published annually in this country, and by 1969 the figure had spiraled to over 7,000 new books and new editions. Many of these titles have made available worthwhile and popular books at a very low price for mass consumption, serving a new book market. However, aside from price, the principal difference between hardcover and paperbound editions is that the paperbound printings are so large that it is necessary to assure a quick sale (as magazines have) on the newsstands where they are generally sold. To achieve such sale, many have been given the "mass-appeal" treatment of vulgar and lurid covers, some of which have little, if any, connection with the contents of the book. Some are in questionable taste; others are certainly not suitable for children, but are readily accessible to them because of their easy proximity and low price. Thus paperbound books have been particularly vulnerable to the local censors' attacks.

In the spring of 1961, an Oklahoma City group called Mothers United For Decency hired a trailer, dubbed it a "smutmobile" and set up an interior display of paperbound books they deemed objectionable. The "smutmobile" was pointedly parked in front of the State Legislature building and thrown open to the adult public. Among the paperbacks on view inside were *Lust for Life, Sons and Lovers, Tobacco Road, God's Little Acre* and *Male and Female* by Margaret Mead.

At least four Chicago paperback outlets were involved in a 1962 three-month, one-woman crusade against smut. The deeply religious mother of a grown son and teenage daughter was eventually arrested for gluing shut the pages of dozens of paperbacks she felt should not be opened by children.

In 1963 the Supreme Court made clear the minimum condition under which a state or local censorship committee's or commission's activities can remotely be considered constitutional. The case centered around a Rhode Island statute which three years earlier had created a Commission to Encourage Morality in Youth. The Commission issued lists of publications considered harmful to youth, with the result that books were removed from sale without adjudication of whether or not they were in fact obscene. Four paperback publishers challenged the Rhode Island system through two rounds in the state courts and into the Supreme Court, which ruled the censorship activities of the Commission unconstitutional in an 8–1 decision. The majority opinion stated: "We are not the first court to look through forms to the substance and recognize that informal censorship may sufficiently inhibit the circulation of publications to warrant injunctive relief. . . . It would be naïve to credit the State's assertion that these blacklists are in the nature of mere legal advice, when they plainly serve as instruments of regulation independent of the laws against obscenity." A commission such as the Rhode Island one, the Court concluded, must at the very least be under direct supervision of the judiciary, and judicial review of such a commission's decisions must be immediately available.

TEXTBOOK CENSORSHIP

The question of the censorship of textbooks used in the public schools in recent years has not been so much one of banning as of rejection or disapproval of certain texts due to the activities of pressure groups.

In the 1930s and 1940s the charge usually leveled against such texts had been that the books were designed to change the existing social order or to record changes in the American way of life. An outstanding instance was the attack in 1939 by the Advertising Federation of America against Harold O. Rugg's *An Introduction to Problems of American Culture*. Professor Rugg, of Teachers College, Columbia University, was the author of many textbooks, of which more than two million copies had been sold within twenty years. In their campaign against Rugg's textbook, the Federation charged the author with "attacking business from every angle" and sneering "at the ideas and traditions of American democracy, making a subtle plea for abolition of our free enterprise system and the introduction of a new social order based on the principles of collectivism . . ."

In 1940 the National Association of Manufacturers was aroused to action on textbooks and undertook an investigation of some 600 school texts to determine the social viewpoint expressed by the authors. The survey by Ralph West Robey aroused a storm of protest from varied quarters, from the American Historical Association to the Harvard Graduate School of Education. Within fifteen years after these violent discussions practically all the books which featured in the controversies were either out of print or not in general use, but this was not necessarily the result of the furor, since books in these fields become outdated by the passage of time.

For several years the New York City Board of Superintendents banned *The Nation* from its list of approved publications for school libraries. The original ban was imposed in June 1948 because of a series of articles on the Roman Catholic Church by Paul Blanshard, subsequently expanded and published as *American Freedom and Catholic Power.*

During the past two decades, attacks on textbooks have been based frequently on the suspicion of subversive material. In 1952 the Texas State Board of Education authorized the Education Commission to request that each publisher submitting books for adoption state whether the authors, illustrators and editors could qualify under the terms of the state's non-subversive oath.

Ten years later the Birch-like Texans for America were successful in dominating the state's textbook adoption hearings and subsequent legislative hearings. Prominent in the objections raised by Texans for America was favorable mention of the income tax, the TVA, Social Security, unemployment compensation, labor unions, racial integration, General George Marshall, and the Supreme Court.

In 1953 the State Legislature of Alabama adopted an anti-Communist law governing the adoption of textbooks in the state's public schools which was to become effective January 1, 1954. It provided that no textbook "will be adopted . . . without a statement by the publisher or author indicating that the author is or is not a known advocate of Communism or Marxist Socialism." This proved to be a law with which publishers found it impossible to comply, and under the leadership of the American Textbook Publishers Institute, twenty-five textbook publishers joined in a suit against the Alabama State Board of Education and the State Textbook Commission. On May 10, 1954, the Circuit Court of Montgomery County adjudged the act void, unenforceable and in violation of the Fourteenth Amendment of the Constitution of the United States.

UNESCO and the UN Declaration of Human Rights have also come in for criticism. In 1954 in El Paso, Texas, the school board banned the use of a history textbook which printed without comment the UN Declaration of Human Rights and the Declaration of Independence. The State Board of Education, however, rejected a demand to drop the book from its list.

Frank Magruder's *American Government* has frequently been under attack. A campaign against this book was led by the *Educational Reviewer,* a quarterly published by the Conference of American Small Business Organizations. Among the cities where the Magruder book was under fire were Chicago, Houston, Little Rock, and Arlington, Virginia. In Georgia the book was attacked as "unfit for use as a social studies textbook because it advocates strengthening the United Nations Charter."

Publishers' Weekly reported that in 1953, "An Indiana state textbook commissioner achieved international notoriety by urging bans on books about Robin Hood and the Quakers as 'helpful to the Communist policy.' " No action resulted from her efforts.

In 1959 the Daughters of the American Revolution issued their first master list of textbooks, classifying them as "satisfactory" or "unsatisfactory." Only 50 satisfactory books were listed, as opposed to 165 unsatisfactory ones being used in schools at that time. The DAR influence was largely responsible for the 1960 Mississippi legislation which gave Governor Ross Barnett the power to select all of the state's textbooks. Taking up his new responsibilities, the governor urged: "Clean up our textbooks. Our children must be properly informed of the Southern and true American way of life."

Equally emotional are the censors who have operated on other precepts. The constitution of the National Association for the Advancement of Colored People directs local branches to study "material used in the schools and seek to eliminate material therefrom which is racially derogatory." Under this directive, the NAACP has mounted attacks on Stephen Foster songs in music books, sections of history books pertaining to the Civil War, and literature anthologies containing *Huckleberry Finn.*

Like the NAACP, the Anti-Defamation League of B'nai B'rith has sought to eliminate racial stereotypes in school materials. In the past, ADL has opposed school use of *Merchant of Venice* and *Oliver Twist.* On the other hand, the organization has actively urged the inclusion in history texts of more material about mass genocide in Nazi Germany.

STATEMENTS ON FREEDOM OF THE PRESS

From *Areopagitica*
A speech by John Milton for the Liberty of Unlicenced Printing to the Parliament of England London 1644

"THE PRECIOUSNESS OF A GOOD BOOK.—I deny not, but that it is of greatest concernment in the Church and Commonwealth, to have a vigilant eye how Bookes demeane themselves as well as men; and thereafter to confine, imprison, and do sharpest justice on them as malefactors: For Books are not absolutely dead things, but doe contain a potencie of life in them to be as active as that soule was whose progeny they are; nay, they do preserve as in a violl the purest efficacie and extraction of that living intellect that bred them. I know they are as lively, and as vigorously productive, as those fabulous Dragons teeth; and being sown up and down, may chance to spring up armed men. And yet on the other hand unlesse warinesse be us'd, as good almost kill a man as kill a good Book; who kills a man kills a reasonable creature, God's Image; but he who destroyes a good Booke, kills reason itselfe, kills the Image of God, as it were in the eye. Many a man lives a burden to the Earth; but a good Booke is the pretious life-blood of a master spirit, imbalm'd and treasur'd up on purpose to a life beyond life. 'Tis true, no age can restore a life, whereof perhaps there is no great losse; and revolutions of ages doe not oft recover the losse of a rejected truth, for the want of which whole Nations fare the worse. We should be wary therefore what persecution we raise against the living labours of publick men, how we spill that season'd life of man preserv'd and stor'd up in Books; since we see a kind of homicide may be thus committed, sometimes a martyrdome; and if it extend to the whole impression, a kinde of massacre, whereof the execution ends not in the slaying of an elementall life, but strikes at that ethereall and fift(h) essence, the breath of reason itselfe, slaies an immortality rather than a life."

From *On Liberty*
By John Stuart Mill
1859

Who can compute what the world loses in the multitude of promising intellects combined with timid characters, who dare not follow out any bold, vigorous, independent train of thought, lest it should land them in something which would admit of being considered irreligious or immoral? . . . No one can be a great thinker who does not recognize that as a thinker it is his first duty to follow his intellect to whatever conclusions it may lead . . .

From Jefferson's Writings

I have sworn upon the altar of God eternal hostility against every form of tyranny over the mind of man.

Thomas Jefferson. Letter to Benjamin Rush, 1800.

Equal and exact justice to all men, of whatever state or persuasion, religious or political; . . . freedom of religion; freedom of the press; freedom of person under the protection of the habeas corpus; and trials by juries impartially selected,—these principles form the bright constellation which has gone before us, and guided our steps through an age of revolution and reformation.

Thomas Jefferson. First Inaugural Address, 1801.

From Amendments to the Constitution
of The United States
1789

ARTICLE I

Freedom of religion, of speech, of the press, and right of petition. —Congress shall make no law respecting an establishment of religion, or prohibiting the free exercise thereof; or abridging the freedom of speech, or of the press; or the right of the people peaceably to assemble, and to petition the Government for a redress of grievances.

ARTICLE XIV
Section 1.

Citizenship defined; privileges of citizens.—All persons born or naturalized in the United States, and subject to the jurisdiction thereof, are citizens of the United States and of the State wherein they reside. No State shall make or enforce any law which shall abridge the privileges or immunities of citizens of the United States; nor shall any State deprive any person of life, liberty, or property, without due process of law; nor deny to any person within its jurisdiction the equal protection of the laws.

Library Bill of Rights
Adopted by Council of ALA at Atlantic City on June 18, 1948

The Council of the American Library Association reaffirms its belief in the following basic policies which should govern the services of all libraries:

1

As a responsibility of library service, books and other reading matter selected should be chosen for values of interest, information and enlightenment of all the people of the community. In no case should any book be excluded because of the race or nationality, or the political or religious views of the writer.

2

There should be the fullest practicable provision of material presenting all points of view concerning the problems and issues of our times, international, national, and local; and books or other reading matter of sound factual authority should not be proscribed or removed from library shelves because of partisan or doctrinal disapproval.

3

Censorship of books, urged or practiced by volunteer arbiters of morals or political opinion or by organizations that would establish a coercive concept of Americanism, must be challenged by libraries in maintenance of their responsibility to provide public information and enlightenment through the printed word.

4

Libraries should enlist the cooperation of allied groups in the fields of science, of education, and of book publishing in resisting all abridgment of the free access to ideas and full freedom of expression that are the tradition and heritage of Americans.

5

As an institution of education for democratic living, the library should welcome the use of its meeting rooms for socially useful and cultural activities and discussion of current public questions. Such meeting places should be available on equal terms to all groups in the community regardless of the beliefs and affiliations of their members.

By official action of the Council on February 3, 1951, the *LIBRARY BILL OF RIGHTS* shall be interpreted to apply to all materials and media of communication used or collected by libraries.

The President's Letter on Intellectual Freedom *to the ALA Meeting in Annual Convention at Los Angeles 1953*

The White House,
Washington, D.C.
June 24, 1953

Dear Dr. Downs:

Thank you for your letter of June 15. I am glad to know of the annual conference of the American Library Association convening this week, and of the spirit of conscientious citizenship ruling its deliberations.

Our librarians serve the precious liberties of our nation: freedom of inquiry, freedom of the spoken and the written word, freedom of exchange of ideas.

Upon these clear principles, democracy depends for its very life, for they are the great sources of knowledge and enlightenment. And knowledge—full, unfettered knowledge of its own heritage, of freedom's enemies, of the whole world of men and ideas—this knowledge is a free people's surest strength.

The converse is just as surely true. A democracy smugly disdainful of new ideas would be a sick democracy. A democracy chronically fearful of new ideas would be a dying democracy.

For all these reasons, we must in these times be intelligently alert not only to the fanatic cunning of Communist conspiracy—but also to the grave dangers in meeting fanaticism with ignorance. For, in order to fight totalitarians who exploit the ways of freedom to serve their own ends, there are some zealots who—with more wrath than wisdom—would adopt a strangely unintelligent course. They would try to defend freedom by denying freedom's friends the opportunity of studying Communism in its entirety—its plausibilities, its falsities, its weaknesses.

But we know that freedom cannot be served by the devices of the tyrant. As it is an ancient truth that freedom cannot be legislated into existence, so it is no less obvious that freedom cannot be censored into existence. And any who act as if freedom's defenses are to be found in suppression and suspicion and fear confess a doctrine that is alien to America.

The libraries of America are and must ever remain the homes of free, inquiring minds. To them, our citizens—of all ages and races, of all creeds and political persuasions—must ever be able to turn with clear confidence that there they can freely seek the whole truth, unwarped by fashion and uncompromised by expediency. For in such whole and healthy knowledge alone are to be found and understood those majestic truths of man's nature and destiny that prove, to each succeeding generation, the validity of freedom.

Sincerely,
Dwight D. Eisenhower

The Freedom to Read

Concerned about threats to free communication of ideas, more than thirty librarians, publishers, and others conferred at Rye, N.Y., May 2–3, 1953. Luther Evans was chairman. A committee was appointed and instructed to prepare a statement which would be made public. This has since become known as the "Westchester Statement." It was endorsed officially by the American Library Association Council on June 25, 1953. It has also the official approval of the American Book Publishers Council, the American Booksellers Association, the Defense Commission of the National Education Association and other national organizations. Its text reads:

"The freedom to read is essential to our democracy. It is under attack. Private groups and public authorities in various parts of the country are working to remove books from sale, to censor textbooks, to label 'controversial' books, to distribute lists of 'objectionable' books or authors, and to purge libraries. These actions apparently rise from a view that our national tradition of free expression is no longer valid; that censorship and suppression are needed to avoid the subversion of politics and the corruption of morals. We, as citizens devoted to the use of books and as librarians and publishers responsible for disseminating them, wish to assert the public interest in the preservation of the freedom to read.

We are deeply concerned about these attempts at suppression. Most such attempts rest on a denial of the fundamental premise of democracy: that the ordinary citizen, by exercising his critical judgment, will accept the good and reject the bad. The censors, public and private, assume that they should determine what is good and what is bad for their fellow-citizens.

We trust Americans to recognize propaganda, and to reject obscenity. We do not believe they need the help of censors to assist them in this task. We do not believe they are prepared to sacrifice their heritage of a free press in order to be 'protected' against what others think may be bad for them. We believe they still favor free enterprise in ideas and expression.

We are aware, of course, that books are not alone in being subjected to efforts at suppression. We are aware that these efforts are related to a larger pattern of pressures being brought against education, the press, films, radio and television. The problem is not only one of actual censorship. The shadow of fear cast by these pressures leads, we suspect, to an even larger voluntary curtailment of expression by those who seek to avoid controversy.

Such pressure toward conformity is perhaps natural to a time of uneasy change and pervading fear. Especially when so many of our apprehensions are directed against an ideology, the expression of a dissident idea becomes a thing feared in itself, and we tend to move against it as against a hostile deed, with suppression.

And yet suppression is never more dangerous than in such a time of social tension. Freedom has given the United States the elasticity to endure strain. Freedom keeps open the path of novel and creative solutions, and enables change to come by choice. Every silencing of a heresy, every enforcement of an orthodoxy, diminishes the toughness and resilience of our society and leaves it the less able to deal with stress.

Now as always in our history, books are among our greatest instruments of freedom. They are almost the only means for making generally available ideas or manners of expression that can initially command only a small audience. They are the natural medium for the new idea and the untried voice, from which come the original contributions to social growth. They are essential to the extended discussion which serious thought requires, and to the accumulation of knowledge and ideas into organized collections.

We believe that free communication is essential to the preservation of a free society and a creative culture. We believe that these pressures towards conformity present the danger of limiting the range and variety of inquiry and expression on which our democracy and our culture depend. We believe that every American community must jealously guard the freedom to publish and to circulate, in order to preserve its own freedom to read. We believe that publishers and librarians have a profound responsibility to give validity to that freedom to read by making it possible for the reader to choose freely from a variety of offerings.

The freedom to read is guaranteed by the Constitution. Those with faith in free men will stand firm on these constitutional guarantees of essential rights and will exercise the responsibilities that accompany these rights.

We therefore affirm these propositions:

1. *It is in the public interest for publishers and librarians to make available the widest diversity of views and expressions, including those which are unorthodox or unpopular with the majority.*

Creative thought is by definition new, and what is new is different. The bearer of every new thought is a rebel until his idea is refined and tested. Totalitarian systems attempt to maintain themselves in power by the ruthless suppression of any concept which challenges the established orthodoxy. The power of a democratic system to adapt to change is vastly strengthened by the freedom of its citizens to choose widely from among conflicting opinions offered freely to them. To stifle every non-conformist idea at birth would mark the end of the democratic process. Furthermore, only through the constant activity of weighing and selecting can the democratic mind attain the strength demanded by times like these. We need to know not only what we believe but why we believe it.

2. *Publishers and librarians do not need to endorse every idea or presentation contained in the books they make available. It would conflict with the public interest for them to establish their own political, moral or aesthetic views as the sole standard for determining what books should be published or circulated.*

Publishers and librarians serve the educational process by helping to make available knowledge and ideas required for the growth of the mind and the increase of learning. They do not foster education by imposing as mentors the patterns of their own thought. The people should have the freedom to read and consider a broader range of ideas than those that may be held by any single librarian or publisher or government or church. It is wrong that what one man can read should be confined to what another thinks proper.

3. *It is contrary to the public interest for publishers or librarians to determine the acceptability of a book solely on the basis of the personal history or political affiliations of the author.*

A book should be judged as a book. No art or literature can flourish if it is to be measured by the political views or private lives of its creators. No society of free men can flourish which draws up lists of writers to whom it will not listen, whatever they may have to say.

4. *The present laws dealing with obscenity should be vigorously enforced. Beyond that, there is no place in our society for extra-legal efforts to coerce the taste of others, to confine adults to the reading matter deemed suitable for adolescents, or to inhibit the efforts of writers to achieve artistic expression.*

To some, much of modern literature is shocking. But is not much of life itself shocking? We cut off literature at the source if we prevent serious artists from dealing with the stuff of life. Parents and teachers have a responsibility to prepare the young to meet the diversity of experiences in life to which they will be exposed, as they have a responsibility to help them learn to think critically for themselves. These are affirmative responsibilities, not discharged simply by preventing them from reading works for which they are not yet prepared. In these matters taste differs, and taste cannot be legislated; nor can machinery be devised which will suit the demands of one group without limiting the freedom of others. We deplore the catering to the immature, the retarded, or the maladjusted taste. But those concerned with freedom have the responsibility of seeing to it that each individual book or publication, whatever its contents, price, or method of distribution, is dealt with in accordance with due process of law.

5. *It is not in the public interest to force a reader to accept with any book the prejudgment of a label characterizing the book or author as subversive or dangerous.*

The idea of labelling supposes the existence of individuals or groups with wisdom to determine by authority what is good or bad for the citizen. It supposes that each individual must be directed in making up his mind about the ideas he examines. But Americans do not need others to do their thinking for them.

6. *It is the responsibility of publishers and librarians, as guardians of the people's freedom to read, to contest encroachments upon that freedom by individuals or groups seeking to impose their own standards or tastes upon the community at large.*

It is inevitable in the give and take of the democratic process that the political, the moral, or the aesthetic concepts of an individual or group will occasionally collide with those of another individual or group. In a free society each individual is free to determine for himself what he wishes to read, and each group is free to determine what it will recommend to its freely associated members. But no group has the right to take the law into its own hands, and to impose its own concepts of politics or morality upon other members of a democratic society. Freedom is no freedom if it is accorded only to the accepted and the inoffensive.

7. *It is the responsibility of publishers and librarians to give full meaning to the freedom to read by providing books that enrich the quality of thought and expression. By the exercise of this affirmative responsibility, bookmen can demonstrate that the answer to a bad book is a good one, the answer to a bad idea is a good one.*

The freedom to read is of little consequence when expended on the trivial; it is frustrated when the reader cannot obtain matter fit for his purpose. What is needed is not only the absence of restraint, but the positive provision of opportunity for the people to read the best that can be thought and said. Books are the major channel by which the intellectual inheritance is handed down, and the principal means of its testing and growth. The defense of their freedom and integrity, and the enlargement of their service to society, requires of all bookmen the utmost of their faculties, and deserves of all citizens the fullest of their support.

We state these propositions neither lightly nor as easy generalizations. We here stake out a lofty claim for the value of books. We do so because we believe that they are good, possessed of enormous variety and usefulness, worthy of cherishing and keeping free. We realize that the application of these propositions may mean the dissemination of ideas and manners of expression that are repugnant to many persons. We do not state these propositions in the comfortable belief that what people read is unimportant. We believe rather that what people read is deeply important; that ideas can be dangerous; but that the suppression of ideas is fatal to a democratic society. Freedom itself is a dangerous way of life, but it is ours."

The members of this drafting committee and signers of "The Freedom to Read" were Luther Evans, Librarian of Congress; ALA President Robert Downs, librarian, University of Illinois; Douglas Black, president, Doubleday & Co.; Arthur Houghton, Jr., president, Steuben Glass; Harold Lasswell, professor of law and political science, Yale Law School; John M. Cory, chief, Circulation Department, New York Public Library; William Dix, chairman, ALA Committee on Intellectual Freedom, and librarian, Princeton University; and Dan Lacy, managing director, ABPC.

Signers of the statement, in addition to those who prepared it were: Bernard Berelson, director, Behavioral Sciences division, Ford Foundation; Mrs. Barry Bingham, Louisville *Courier-Journal;* Paul Bixler, librarian, Antioch College; Charles G. Bolté, executive secretary, ABPC; Cass Canfield, chairman, Harper & Bros., member, ABPC Committee on Reading Development; Robert Carr, professor of law and politics, Dartmouth; David H. Clift, executive secretary, ALA; Harold K. Guinzburg, president, Viking Press, chairman ABPC Committee on Reading Development; Richard Barnes Kennan, secretary, Commission for the Defense of Democracy through Education, National Education Association; Chester Kerr, secretary, Yale University Press, chairman, Committee on Freedom to Publish, Association of American University Presses; Lloyd King, executive secretary, American Textbook Publishers Institute; Donald S. Klopfer, secretary and treasurer, Random House, chairman, ABPC Anti-Censorship Committee; Alfred A. Knopf, president, Alfred A. Knopf, Inc.; David E. Lilienthal, lawyer; Milton Lord, librarian, Boston Public Library; Flora Belle Ludington, librarian, Mt. Holyoke College, newly-installed president, ALA; Horace Manges, counsel, ABPC; Ralph McGill, editor, Atlanta *Constitution;* Robert K. Merton, professor of sociology, Columbia; John O'Connor, president, Grosset & Dunlap, immediate past president, ABPC; Leo Rosten, author; A. Ruth Rutzen, director, Home Reading Services, Detroit Public Library; Francis St. John, librarian, Brooklyn Public Library; Whitney North Seymour, former president, Association of the Bar of the City of New York; Theodore Waller, editorial vice-president, New American Library, former managing director, ABPC; Bethuel M. Webster, Association of the Bar of the City of New York, counsel, the Fund for the Republic; Victor Weybright, chairman and editor, NAL, chairman, ABPC Reprinters Committee; Thomas J. Wilson, director, Harvard University Press, immediate past president, AAUP.

MORRIS L. ERNST
ON BANNED BOOKS

The following text, which Morris Ernst wrote as an introduction to the second edition of Banned Books, *is being reprinted not so much for its statement on this work as for its thought-provoking commentary on the subject at large.*

The compiler of this work, a widened version of the original volume published in 1935, has made a major contribution to Freedom for Books. Any one who looks over the list of banned books, even casually, must, in the first instance, ask what could have frightened man to suppress books such as "Gulliver's Travels," in Ireland considered obscene and detrimental to both government and morals; Hans Christian Andersen's "Wonder Stories," banned by Nicholas I of Russia, who also suppressed "Uncle Tom's Cabin" and "The Scarlet Letter"; or Jack London's "The Call of the Wild," banned as radical in Italy and Yugoslavia in 1929. In a world where practically everyone has the answers, I am sure that this is one time when the right questions are more important than the answers. Mrs. Haight's volume must, in the minds of all people of good will, raise fundamental queries: Have man's fears ever been valid? Why should we trust a government or a church to control our literary diet after we have seen the validity of the former fears of those in power? Are we not better off trusting the people of our nation to accept or reject books in the market place of thought? Have we not staked our all on a gamble, not yet empirically provable, and hence calling for an act of faith, that truth has a better chance of winning out in an open market place of thought rather than by controls placed in the hands of rulers whether ecclesiastical or secular?

We scarcely need additional exhortations such as Milton's "Areopagitica" on the theory of freedom of thought in view of the evidence presented in this volume. Aside from the scientific inquiries undertaken in recent years to discover what effect the printed word has on the people of our nation, the matrix of Mrs. Haight's work proves that any guess as to the danger of ideas at any moment of history looks silly and vapid in the next decades. Even though truth crushed to earth will rise again, the crushing process is unbecoming for free people and may well delay that wholesome march of man toward the development of his potential joys and powers, potentials of the future scarcely discernible at any single moment of history.

We know little about man's ultimate potentials. But one of the brakes preventing man's realization of his potentials may be the failure to explore the roots of man's fear of ideas. Happily, science is now directing its attention in that area. I have always believed that the pen has more might than the sword because throughout man's history the sword has been used to kill even the wielders of the pen; but the words and ideas had the capacity of secret survival or re-birth. For centuries man was most afraid, and hence tried to suppress criticism of the church or its dogma—called blasphemy. Marc Con-nelly's innocuous and charming play "Green Pastures" was banned in England and Norway because it showed God on the stage. The first edition of Lena Towsley's "Peter and Peggy" was stopped here because the children were not shown saying their prayers. And Dante's "Divine Comedy" was burned in France in 1318, and fell under the Inquisition in Lisbon in 1581. The Spanish Inquisition banned Francis Bacon's "Advancement of Learning."

The church, maintaining power over masses of illiterate folk, gave evidence of its inner insecurity by endeavoring to maintain power by the suppression of criticism or even diversity of religious opinion. As the power of the church was diminished through the developing sovereignty of the state the insecurity, the fear and hence the censorship shifted from blasphemy into the area of sedition, and then after the democratic process had taken root as opposed to a royal sovereignty the power of the state over man's minds dwindled. And still men and women had to fill their censorious requirements and did so by creating the next big shift, that is, from criticism of the state to references to sex, or in legal terms, from sedition to ob-scenity.

Literary obscenity is the newest toy of the frightened, and obvi-ously varies among cultures depending upon the sexual folkways. Few sophisticated cultures are free of this fear. In sophisticated cul-tures the official standards for sexual behavior are as a rule far more rigid and more prudish than the actual practices of the people. No doubt there were a few Greeks who disapproved of homosexuality, lesbianism and infanticide which were all practiced openly; just as among the Jews some may have rejected the world of Solomon and his many wives. I mention these two cultures since our folkway seems to me to have incorporated antithetical features of each. In any event the gap between standards and practices reveals the cen-sorious sexual anxieties of a country.

In 16th Century England, Sir Thomas Malory's "The Birth, Life and Acts of King Arthur" was denounced as "bold adultery and wilful murder." The first printed book to be banned in England was the Tyndale Bible, not for blasphemy but because of Henry VIII's sensitiveness on the subject of divorce. Louis XVI considered Beaumarchais' "Le Mariage de Figaro" immoral; and Boston withdrew from publication Whitman's "Leaves of Grass."

With the advent of Mussolini, Hitler and Stalin, a combination of fears—obscenity and sedition—crept into the national patterns. Dictators fear and hence create fears. In Spain under Franco, the twin fears seem to be blasphemy and obscenity. In our own Republic at this time we find two fears, one known as McCarthyism and the other an apparent spurt in the drive against sexual material in books, a drive which apparently exempts the daily press.

Since 1900, two important events have taken place that touch on man's fear of ideas. From the days of vellum and quill through Gutenberg and up to the turn of the 20th Century, ideas could reach the minds of people only through speech, writing or printing. During the past fifty years new media have developed—radio, movies and television. Each new medium created new fears. Nevertheless, the persistent pattern continued; the censors who read for sedition, blasphemy or obscenity never felt that they themselves would be corrupted. They were only worried for the souls of others.

This development happened to coincide with new exciting explorations, in scientific terms, of what effect ideas have on men, women or children. Are the effects of the different media comparable? We already know that women are differently affected by sexual writings than are men and there is some reason to believe that children are less affected by fiction than by reality.

Despite random comment of loose-tongued, frightened people, there is as yet little reason to believe that the written word has a provable causal relation to behavior. However, I suspect that the effect, if any, is more often in the direction of acts of omission than commission. For example, a "good" girl reads about the Fairy Prince, who fails to appear for her. So unwilling to marry a lesser Prince, she lives out her life in needless solitary virginity! Despite the new media there is substantial and increasing agreement that books are the prime enduring source of man's continuing culture. Material flowing over the ether or appearing in the daily newspapers is ephemeral and particularly in our folkway people are apt to say, implying a deviation from fact, "it is only a newspaper story."

Any subject that deals with man's fears or even with his potential hopes should be placed in its historical background. In the main, this volume is concerned not with the open adverse public criticism in the market place of thought as to any particular volume, but with the exercise of sovereignty, whether by church or state, to suppress ideas. In this connection, much of the trouble in our Republic derives from the inaccurate education of our people as to our proud and expanding Bill of Rights. We have adopted the myth that the Founding Fathers were against censorship and that the First Amendment to the Constitution guaranteed freedom of thought. Nothing can be further from the truth. When the Twelve Colonies (Rhode Island failed to appear) banded together in the Convention of Philadelphia in 1787, not a word was mentioned, during those great four months, on the subject of freedom of the press. Our Constitution is silent on the subject. The First Amendment, which is probably the greatest contribution of our nation to the history of government, was inserted only because the States wanted to make sure that the new Federal Government would keep its hands off the censorship business and would leave the entire control over the minds of the people in the hands of the state governments. Such was the pattern of our nation until around 1920 when the Supreme Court of the United States for the first time held that even the states could no longer abridge freedom of the press. While the daily newspapers early attained a status free from persistent governmental interference, the movies supinely begged for governmental pre-censorship. Radio and television, as well as movies, fended off governmental controls by horizontal industrial agreements which vitally and, in my opinion, illegally restrict the market place of thought and the intellectual diet of our people.

An odd footnote on one of our present areas of fear. For eighty years, that is up to 1870, there was practically no legislation banning that indefinable subject known as obscenity. After debate of a few minutes in each house of the Congress, a frightened neurotic by the name of Anthony Comstock, playing on the sex hypocrisy of our folkways, pushed through our first obscenity laws, promptly to be copied in most of the states of the Union. From 1870 to 1915, the practice of book publishers was to submit manuscripts to the Comstock society. This period, known as the "dark age of books," ended when a few publishers believed that freedom and profits were not antithetical, and during the two decades after 1915 a line of cases were brought to court narrowing to a substantial extent suppressible obscenity. It has been my privilege and joy to participate in many of these cases. Since the great decision of Judge Woolsey in the "Ulysses" case, it has become increasingly clear that no book openly published, openly distributed and publicly reviewed would be denied distribution to our people if the publisher and author did battle with the censors in stout and brave terms, but in recent years the book publishers have become increasingly timid and have compromised away much of their liberty, thus inviting into the American mores a mass of local ordinances and state laws and local undisclosed pressure groups. It is my best judgment that at no time in our national history have books been so pushed around, this despite valiant efforts by the association of book publishers, groups of authors and librarians. And may I add that in historic terms the frightened mob only chases those who run. Indeed, it may be good for man that he must learn to dig his heels in the ground, at which gesture the mob ordinarily fails to advance.

This book will help all who read it to dig their heels in the ground —having read the historical evidence of man's prior invalid fears of his most precious commodity—ideas.

EXCERPTS FROM
IMPORTANT COURT DECISIONS

Excerpt from the Opinion of Alexander Cockburn,
Lord Chief Justice of England
Queen vs. Hicklin *and* The Confessional Unmasked,
1868 (Known as the Hicklin rule on obscenity)

"I think the test of obscenity is this, whether the tendency of the matter charged as obscenity is to deprave and corrupt those whose minds are open to such immoral influences, and into whose hands a publication of this sort may fall."

Excerpts from the Opinion of Judge Learned Hand
United States vs. Mitchell Kennerley *and* Hagar
Revelly *United States District Court of Southern*
New York, 1913
(Protest against the Hicklin rule)

". . . I hope it is not improper for me to say that the rule as laid down, however consonant it may be with mid-Victorian morals, (Cockburn opinion) does not seem to me to answer to the understanding and morality of the present time . . . I question whether in the end men will regard that as obscene which is honestly relevant to the adequate expression of innocent ideas, and whether they will not believe that truth and beauty are too precious to society at large to be mutilated in the interests of those most likely to pervert them to base uses. Indeed, it seems hardly likely that we are even to-day so lukewarm in our interest in letters or serious discussion as to be content to reduce our treatment of sex to the standard of a child's library in the supposed interest of a salacious few, or that shame will for long prevent us from adequate portrayal of some of the most serious and beautiful sides of human nature . . .

"Yet, if the time is not yet when men think innocent all that which is honestly germane to a pure subject, however little it may mince its words, still I scarcely think that they would forbid all which might corrupt the most corruptible, or that society is prepared to accept for its own limitations those which may perhaps be necessary to the weakest of its members. If there be no abstract definition, such as I have suggested, should not the word 'obscene' be allowed to indicate the present critical point in the compromise between candor and shame at which the community may have arrived here and now? . . . To put thought in leash to the average conscience of the time is perhaps tolerable, but to fetter it by the necessities of the lowest and least capable seems a fatal policy."

Excerpts from the Opinion of Judge John Woolsey United States vs. Ulysses and Random House, Inc. U.S. District Court, Southern District of New York, December 6, 1933

. . . "in any case where a book is claimed to be obscene it must first be determined, whether the intent with which it was written was what is called, according to the usual phrase, pornographic,—that is, written for the purpose of exploiting obscenity.

. . . But in *Ulysses,* in spite of its unusual frankness, I do not detect anywhere the leer of the sensualist. I hold, therefore, that it is not pornographic.

. . . although it contains . . . many words usually considered dirty, I have not found anything that I consider to be dirt for dirt's sake.

. . . when such a real artist in words, as Joyce undoubtedly is, seeks to draw a true picture of the lower middle class in a European city, ought it to be impossible for the American public legally to see that picture?

. . . The statute under which the libel is filed only denounces, in so far as we are here concerned, the importation into the United States from any foreign country of 'any obscene book'.

. . . The meaning of the word 'obscene' as legally defined by the Courts is: tending to stir the sex impulses or to lead to sexually impure and lustful thoughts.

. . . Whether a particular book would tend to excite such impulses and thoughts must be tested by the Court's opinion as to its effect on a person with average sex instincts.

. . . It is only with the normal person that the law is concerned

. . . a book like *Ulysses* . . . is a sincere and serious attempt to devise a new literary method for the observation and description of mankind.

. . . I am quite aware that owing to some of its scenes *Ulysses* is a rather strong draught to ask some sensitive, though normal, persons to take. But my considered opinion, after long reflection, is that whilst in many places the effect of *Ulysses* on the reader undoubtedly is somewhat emetic, no where does it tend to be an aphrodisiac. *Ulysses* may, therefore, be admitted into the United States."

Excerpts from the Opinion of Judge Augustus N. Hand
New York Circuit Court of Appeals
On an appeal of the Ulysses case, 1934

"While any construction of the statute that will fit all cases is difficult, we believe that the proper test of whether a given book is obscene is its dominant effect. In applying this test, relevancy of the objectionable parts to the theme, the established reputation of the work in the estimation of approved critics, if the book is modern, and the verdict of the past, if it is ancient, are persuasive pieces of evidence; for works of art are not likely to sustain a high position with no better warrant for their existence than their obscene content."

Excerpts from the Opinion of Judge Curtis Bok
State of Pennsylvania vs. Five Booksellers
Court of Quarter Sessions, Philadelphia,
March 18, 1949

. . . "I hold that Section 524 may not constitutionally be applied to any writing unless it is sexually impure and pornographic. It may then be applied, as an exercise of the police power, only where there is a reasonable and demonstrable cause to believe that a crime or misdemeanor has been committed or is about to be committed as the perceptible result of the publication and distribution of the writing in question: the opinion of anyone that a tendency thereto exists or that such a result is self-evident is insufficient and irrelevant. The casual connection between the book and the criminal behavior must appear beyond a reasonable doubt.
. . . There is no such proof in the instant case.
. . . Section 524, for all its verbiage, is very bare. The full weight of the legislative prohibition dangles from the word 'obscene' and its synonyms. Nowhere are these words defined; nowhere is the danger to be expected of them stated; nowhere is a standard of judgment set forth. I assume that 'obscenity' is expected to have a familiar and inherent meaning, both as to what it is and as to what it does.

It is my purpose to show that it has no such inherent meaning; that different meanings given to it at different times are not constant, either historically or legally; and that it is not constitutionally indictable unless it takes the form of sexual impurity, i.e., 'dirt for dirt's sake' and can be traced to actual criminal behavior, either actual or demonstrably imminent.

. . . I believe that the consensus of preference today is for disclosure and not stealth, for frankness and not hypocrisy, and for public and not secret distribution. That in itself is a moral code.

It is my opinion that frank disclosure cannot legally be censored, even as an exercise of the police power, unless it is sexually impure and pornographic.

. . . Who can define the clear and present danger to the community that arises from reading a book? If we say it is that the reader is young and inexperienced and incapable of resisting the sexual temptations that the book may present to him, we put the entire reading public at the mercy of the adolescent mind and of those adolescents who do not have the expected advantages of home influence, school training, or religious teaching. Nor can we say into how many such hands the book may come. . . . If the argument be applied to the general public, the situation becomes absurd, for then no publication is safe. . . ."

Excerpts from the Opinion of the U.S. Supreme Court Roth vs. United States June 24, 1957

. . . All ideas having even the slightest redeeming social importance —unorthodox ideas, controversial ideas, even ideas hateful to the prevailing climate of opinion—have the full protection of the guaranties, unless excludable because they encroach upon the limited area of more important interests. But implicit in the history of the First Amendment is the rejection of obscenity as utterly without redeeming social importance. This rejection for that reason is mirrored in the universal judgment that obscenity should be restrained, reflected in the international agreement of over 50 nations, in the obscenity laws of all of the 48 states, and in the 20 obscenity laws enacted by the Congress from 1842 to 1956. . . . We hold that obscenity is not within the area of constitutionally protected speech or press.

. . . However, sex and obscenity are not synonymous. Obscene material is material which deals with sex in a manner appealing to prurient interest. The portrayal of sex, *e.g.,* in art, literature and scientific works, is not itself sufficient reason to deny material the constitutional protection of freedom of speech and press. Sex, a great and mysterious motive force in human life, has indisputably been a subject of absorbing interest to mankind through the ages; it is one of the vital problems of human interest and public concern.

UNITED STATES CUSTOMS AND POSTAL LAWS AND REGULATIONS

Covering the Importation, Transportation and
Mailing of Books and Other Printed Material.

TARIFF ACT OF 1930. 46 Stat. 688; 19 U.S.C. 1305
SECTION 305
Immoral articles; importation prohibited.

(a) All persons are prohibited from importing into the United States from any foreign country any book, pamphlet, paper, writing, advertisement, circular, print, picture, or drawing containing any matter advocating or urging treason or insurrection against the United States, or forcible resistance to any law of the United States, or containing any threat to take the life of or inflict bodily harm upon any person in the United States, or any obscene book, pamphlet, paper, writing, advertisement, circular, print, picture, drawing, or other representation, figure, or image on or of paper or other material, or any cast, instrument, or other article which is obscene or immoral, or any drug or medicine or any article whatever for the prevention of conception or for causing unlawful abortion, or any lottery ticket, or any printed paper that may be used as a lottery ticket, or any advertisement of any lottery. No such articles, whether imported separately or contained in packages with other goods entitled to entry, shall be admitted to entry; and all such articles and, unless it appears to the satisfaction of the collector that the obscene or other prohibited articles contained in the package were inclosed therein without the knowledge or consent of the importer, owner, agent, or consignee, the entire contents of the package in which such articles are contained, shall be subject to seizure and forfeiture as hereinafter provided: *Provided,* That the drugs hereinbefore mentioned, when imported in bulk and not put up for any of the purposes hereinbefore specified, are excepted from the operation of this subdivision: *Provided further,* That the Secretary of the Treasury may, in his discretion, admit the so-called classics or books of recognized and established literary or scientific merit, but may, in his discretion, admit such classics or books only when imported for noncommercial purposes.

Upon the appearance of any such book or matter at any customs office, the same shall be seized and held by the collector to await the judgment of the district court as hereinafter provided; and no protest shall be taken to the United States Customs Court from the decision of the collector. Upon the seizure of such book or matter the collector shall transmit information thereof to the district attorney of the district in which is situated the office at which such seizure has taken place, who shall institute proceedings in the district court for the forfeiture, confiscation, and destruction of the book or matter seized. Upon the adjudication that such book or matter thus seized is of the character the entry of which is by this section prohibited, it shall be ordered destroyed and shall be destroyed. Upon adjudication that such book or matter thus seized is not of the character the entry of which is by this section prohibited, it shall not be excluded from entry under the provisions of this section.

In any such proceeding any party in interest may upon demand have the facts at issue determined by a jury and any party may have an appeal or the right of review as in the case of ordinary actions or suits.

62 Stat. 718; 18 U.S.C. 552 (replacing subparagraph (b)
of Section 305 of Tariff Act)
*Officers aiding importation of obscene or treasonous
books and articles.*

Whoever, being an officer, agent, or employee of the United States knowingly aids or abets any person engaged in any violation of any of the provisions of law prohibiting importing, advertising, dealing in, exhibiting, or sending or receiving by mail obscene or indecent publications or representations, or books, pamphlets, papers, writings, advertisements, circulars, prints, pictures, or drawings containing any matter advocating or urging treason or insurrection against the United States or forcible resistance to any law of the United States, or containing any threat to take the life of or inflict bodily harm upon any person in the United States, or means for preventing conception or procuring abortion, or other articles of indecent or immoral use or tendency, shall be fined not more than $5,000 or imprisoned not more than ten years, or both.

CUSTOMS REGULATIONS

*12.40 Seizure; disposition of seized articles; reports to
United States attorney.*

(a) Any book, pamphlet, paper, writing, advertisement, circular, print, picture, or drawing containing any matter advocating or urging treason or insurrection against the United States, or forcible resistance to any law of the United States, or containing any threat to take the life of or inflict bodily harm upon any person in the United States, seized under section 305, Tariff Act of 1930, shall be transmitted to the United States attorney for his consideration and action.

(b) Upon the seizure of articles or matter prohibited entry by section 305, Tariff Act of 1930 (with the exception of the matter described in paragraph (a) of this section), a notice of the seizure of such articles or matter shall be sent to the consignee or addressee.

(c) When articles of the class covered by paragraph (b) of this section are of small value and no criminal intent is apparent, a blank assent to forfeiture and destruction of the articles seized, customs Form 4609, shall be sent with the notice of seizure. Upon receipt of the assent to forfeiture and destruction duly executed, the articles shall be destroyed if not needed for official use and the case closed.

(d) In the case of a repeated offender or when the facts indicate that the importation was made deliberately with intent to evade the law, the facts and evidence shall be submitted to the United States attorney for consideration of prosecution of the offender as well as an action in rem under section 305 for condemnation of the articles.

(e) If the importer declines to execute an assent to forfeiture of the articles other than those mentioned in paragraph (a) of this section and fails to submit, within 30 days after being notified of his privilege so to do, a petition under section 618, Tariff Act of 1930, for the remission of the forefeiture and permission to export the seized merchandise, information concerning the seizure shall be submitted to the United States attorney in accordance with the provisions of the second paragraph of section 305 (a), Tariff Act of 1930, for the institution of condemnation proceedings.

(f) If seizure is made of books or other articles which do not contain obscene matter but contain information or advertisements relative to the prevention of conception or to means of causing abortion, the procedure outlined in paragraphs (b), (c), (d), and (e) of this section shall be followed.

(g) In any case when a book is seized as being obscene and the importer declines to execute an assent to forfeiture on the ground that the book is a classic, or of recognized and established literary or scientific merit, a petition addressed to the Secretary of the Treasury with evidence to support the claim may be filed by the importer for release of the book. Mere unsupported statements or allegations will not be considered. If the ruling is favorable, release of such book shall be made only to the ultimate consignee.

(h) Whenever it clearly appears from information, instructions, advertisements enclosed with or appearing on any drug or medicine or its immediate or other container, or otherwise that such drug or medicine is intended for preventing conception or inducing abortion, such drug or medicine shall be detained or seized. The mere fact that it may be capable of contraceptive use is not conclusive on the question of intent.

(i) Contraceptive devices imported by or for a particular physician shall not be detained under the provisions of section 305, Tariff Act of 1930, if the collector of customs concerned is satisfied that the ultimate consignee is a reputable physician, and if there is filed with such collector a declaration of the ultimate consignee stating that the devices are to be used only to protect the health of his patients.

(j) When an importer contends that he may lawfully import contraceptive articles and the collector is not satisfied that the importation is within the purview of paragraph (i) of this section, he shall be advised to file with the collector a communication addressed to the Commissioner of Customs setting forth his claims in detail to be transmitted by the collector to the Bureau together with a full report of the facts. Pending the Bureau's decision in such cases, any article consigned to the claimant and believed by the collector to be prohibited from importation shall be detained but not seized.

CRIMES—OBSCENITY

62 Stat. 768; amended 64 Stat. 194; 18 U.S.C. 1462
Importation or transportation of obscene matters.

Whoever brings into the United States, or any place subject to the jurisdiction thereof, or knowingly uses any express company or other common carrier, for carriage in interstate or foreign commerce— (a) any obscene, lewd, lascivious, or filthy book, pamphlet, picture, motion-picture film, paper, letter, writing, print, or other matter of indecent character; or (b) any obscene, lewd, lascivious, or filthy phonograph recording, electrical transcription, or other article or thing capable of producing sounds; or (c) any drug, medicine, article, or thing designed, adapted, or intended for preventing conception, or producing abortion, or for any indecent or immoral use; or any written or printed card, letter, circular, book, pamphlet, advertisement, or notice of any kind giving information directly or indirectly, where, how, or of whom, or by what means any of such mentioned articles, matters, or things may be obtained or made; or

Whoever knowingly takes from such express company or other

common carrier any matter or thing the depositing of which for carriage is herein made unlawful—

Shall be fined not more than $5,000 or imprisoned not more than five years, or both, for the first such offense and shall be fined not more than $10,000 or imprisoned not more than ten years, or both, for each such offense thereafter.

62 Stat. 768; 18 U.S.C. 1461

Mailing obscene or crime-inciting matter.

Every obscene, lewd, lascivious, indecent, filthy or vile article, matter, thing, device, or substance; and—

Every article or thing designed, adapted, or intended for preventing conception or producing abortion, or for any indecent or immoral use; and

Every article, instrument, substance, drug, medicine, or thing which is advertised or described in a manner calculated to lead another to use or apply it for preventing conception or producing abortion, or for any indecent or immoral purpose; and

Every written or printed card, letter, circular, book, pamphlet, advertisement, or notice of any kind giving information, directly or indirectly, where, or how, or from whom, or by what means any of such mentioned matters, articles, or things may be obtained or made, or where or by whom any act or operation of any kind for the procuring or producing of abortion will be done or performed, or how or by what means conception may be prevented or abortion produced, whether sealed or unsealed; and

Every letter, packet, or package, or other mail matter containing any filthy, vile, or indecent thing, device, or substance; and

Every paper, writing, advertisement, or representation that any article, instrument, substance, drug, medicine, or thing may, or can, be used or applied for preventing conception or producing abortion, or for any indecent or immoral purpose; and

Every description calculated to induce or incite a person to so use or apply such article, instrument, substance, drug, medicine, or thing—

Is declared to be nonmailable matter and shall not be conveyed in the mails or delivered from any post office by any letter carrier.

Whoever knowingly uses the mails for the mailing, carriage in the mails, or delivery of anything declared by this section to be nonmailable, or knowingly causes to be delivered by mail according to the direction thereon, or at the place at which it is directed to be delivered to the person to whom it is addressed, or knowingly takes any such thing from the mails for the purpose of circulating or disposing thereof; or of aiding in the circulation or disposition thereof, shall be fined not more than $5,000 or imprisoned not more than five years, or both, for the first such offense, and shall be fined not more than $10,000 or imprisoned not more than ten years, or both, for each such offense thereafter.

The term "indecent," as used in this section, includes matter of a character tending to incite arson, murder, or assassination.

62 Stat. 769; 18 U.S.C. 1463
Mailing indecent matter on wrappers or envelopes.

All matter otherwise mailable by law, upon the envelope or outside cover or wrapper of which, and all postal cards upon which, any delineations, epithets, terms, or language of an indecent, lewd, lascivious, or obscene character are written or printed or otherwise impressed or apparent, are nonmailable matter, and shall not be conveyed in the mails nor delivered from any post office nor by any letter carrier, and shall be withdrawn from the mails under such regulations as the Postmaster General shall prescribe.

Whoever knowingly deposits for mailing or delivery, any thing declared by this section to be nonmailable matter, or knowingly takes the same from the mails for the purpose of circulating or disposing of or aiding in the circulation or disposition of the same, shall be fined not more than $5,000 or imprisoned not more than five years, or both.

CRIMES—POSTAL SERVICE

62 Stat. 782; 18 U.S.C. 1717.
Letters and writings as nonmailable; opening letters.

(a) Every letter, writing, circular, postal card, picture, print, engraving, photograph, newspaper, pamphlet, book, or other publication, matter, or thing, in violation of sections 499, 506, 793, 794, 915, 954, 956, 957, 960, 964, 1017, 1542, 1543, 1544, or 2388 of this title or which contains any matter advocating or urging treason, insurrection, or forcible resistance to any law of the United States is nonmailable and shall not be conveyed in the mails or delivered from any post office or by any letter carrier.

(b) Whoever uses or attempts to use the mails or Postal Service of the United States for the transmission of any matter declared by this section to be nonmailable, shall be fined not more than $5,000 or imprisoned not more than ten years, or both.

REGULATION OF PROPAGANDISTS

52 Stat. 631; 53 Stat. 1244; 56 Stat. 248; 60 Stat. 1352;
64 Stat. 1005; 22 U.S.C. 611 (j)

Definitions

As used in and for the purpose of this subchapter

(j) The term "political propaganda" includes any oral, visual, graphic, written, pictorial, or other communication or expression by any person (1) which is reasonably adapted to, or which the person disseminating the same believes will, or which he intends to, prevail upon, indoctrinate, convert, induce, or in any other way influence a recipient or any section of the public within the United States with reference to the political or public interests, policies, or relations of a government of a foreign country or a foreign political party or with reference to the foreign policies of the United States or promote in the United States racial, religious, or social dissensions, or (2) which advocates, advises, instigates, or promotes any racial, social, political, or religious disorder, civil riot, or other conflict involving the use of force or violence in any other American republic or the overthrow of any government or political subdivision of any other American republic by any means involving the use of force or violence. As used in this subsection the term "disseminating" includes transmitting or causing to be transmitted in the United States mails or by any means or instrumentality of interstate or foreign commerce or offering or causing to be offered in the United States mails.

56 Stat. 257 64 Stat. 1005; 22 U.S.C. 618 (d)

Enforcement and Penalties.

(d) The Postmaster General may declare to be nonmailable any communication or expression falling within clause (2) of section 611 (j) of this title in the form of prints or in any other form reasonably adapted to, or reasonably appearing to be intended for, dissemination or circulation among two or more persons, which is offered or caused to be offered for transmittal in the United States mails to any person or persons in any other American republic by any agent of a foreign principal, if the Postmaster General is informed in writing by the Secretary of State that the duly accredited diplomatic representative of such American republic has made written representation to the Department of State that the admission or circulation of such communication or expression in such American republic is prohibited by the laws thereof and has requested in writing that its transmittal thereto be stopped.

52 Stat. 632; 53 Stat. 1246; 56 Stat. 255; 22 U.S.C. 614

Filing and labeling of political propaganda.

(a) Every person within the United States who is an agent of a foreign principal and required to register under the provisions of this subchapter and who transmits or causes to be transmitted in the United States mails or by any means or instrumentality of interstate or foreign commerce any political propaganda for or in the interests of such foreign principal (i) in the form of prints, or (ii) in any other form which is reasonably adapted to being, or which he believes will be, or which he intends to be, disseminated or circulated among two or more persons shall, not later than forty-eight hours after the beginning of the transmittal thereof, file with the Attorney General two copies thereof and a statement, duly signed by or on behalf of such agent, setting forth full information as to the places, times, and extent of such transmittal.

(b) It shall be unlawful for any person within the United States who is an agent of a foreign principal and required to register under the provisions of this subchapter to transmit or cause to be transmitted in the United States mails or by any means or instrumentality of interstate or foreign commerce any political propaganda for or in the interests of such foreign principal (i) in the form of prints, or (ii) in any other form which is reasonably adapted to being, or which he believes will be or which he intends to be, disseminated or circulated among two or more persons, unless such political propaganda is conspicuously marked at its beginning with, or prefaced or accompanied by, a true and accurate statement, in the language or languages used in such political propaganda, setting forth the relationship or connection between the person transmitting the political propaganda or causing it to be transmitted and such propaganda; that the person transmitting such political propaganda or causing it to be transmitted is registered under this subchapter with the Department of Justice, Washington, District of Columbia, as an agent of a foreign principal, together with the name and address of such agent of a foreign principal and of each of his foreign principals; that, as required by this subchapter, his registration statement is available for inspection at and copies of such political propaganda are being filed with the Department of Justice; and that registration of agents of foreign principals required by the subchapter does not indicate approval by the United States Government of the contents of their political propaganda. The Attorney General, having due regard for the national security and the public interest, may by regulation prescribe the language or languages and the manner and form in which such statement shall be made and require the inclusion of such other information contained in the registration statement identifying such agent of a foreign principal and such political propaganda and its sources as may be appropriate.

(c) The copies of political propaganda required by this subchapter to be filed with the Attorney General shall be available for public inspection under such regulations as he may prescribe.

(d) For purposes of the Library of Congress, other than for public distribution, the Secretary of the Treasury and the Postmaster General are authorized, upon the request of the Librarian of Congress, to forward to the Library of Congress fifty copies, or as many fewer thereof as are available, of all foreign prints determined to be prohibited entry under the provisions of section 1305 of Title 19 and of all foreign prints excluded from the mails under authority of section 343 of Title 18.

Notwithstanding the provisions of section 1305 of Title 19 and of section 343 of Title 18, the Secretary of the Treasury is authorized to permit the entry and the Postmaster General is authorized to permit the transmittal in the mails of foreign prints imported for governmental purposes by authority or for the use of the United States or for the use of the Library of Congress.

(e) It shall be unlawful for any person within the United States who is an agent of a foreign principal required to register under the provisions of this subchapter to transmit, convey, or otherwise furnish to any agency or official of the Government (including a Member or committee of either House of Congress) for or in the interests of such foreign principal any political propaganda or to request from any such agency or official for or in the interests of such foreign principal any information or advice with respect to any matter pertaining to the political or public interests, policies or relations of a foreign country or of a political party or pertaining to the foreign or domestic policies of the United States unless the propaganda or the request is prefaced or accompanied by a true and accurate statement to the effect that such person is registered as an agent of such foreign principal under this subchapter.

(f) Whenever any agent of a foreign principal required to register under this subchapter appears before any committee of Congress to testify for or in the interests of such foreign principal, he shall, at the time of such appearance, furnish the committee with a copy of his most recent registration statement filed with the Department of Justice as an agent of such foreign principal for inclusion in the records of the committee as part of his testimony.

ATTORNEY GENERAL'S OPINION. 39 Op. Atty. Gen. 535, 1940

An opinion by the Attorney General on December 10, 1940 upon a question submitted by the Postmaster General in respect to the Foreign Agents' Registration Act of 1938 has been utilized by the Post Office Department as its legal basis for declaring non-mailable political propaganda mailed by an agent of a foreign principal outside the United States to persons within the United States, and as a basis upon which the Bureau of Customs is resting its authority for the seizure of propaganda material arriving in the United States by freight or express from agents of foreign principals located outside the United States and destined to persons not registered with the Department of Justice. The Attorney General's ruling was to the effect that if the mailed matter involved is of such a character that distributors of it in this country would be subject to the provisions of the Foreign Agents' Registration Act of June 18, 1938, and if the foreign mailers have not complied with the requirement of registration, exclusion from the United States mails would be authorized.

POSTAL MANUAL

A revised edition of the *Postal Manual* was issued in the fall of 1954, consolidating postal regulations and procedures including those affecting nonmailable matter (Part 124). Copies can be obtained from the Superintendent of Documents, Government Printing Office, Washington 25, D.C. for 65¢. This is the first revision of the *Postal Manual* since the Post Office Department was founded and has been written in language which the layman can understand.

BIBLIOGRAPHY

The bibliography that follows is far from exhaustive. It is merely a guide to some of the interesting and currently more useful works on the subject. Readers who wish to delve deeply into censorship are advised to consult the splendid and fascinating work by Ralph E. McCoy: Freedom of the Press, an annotated bibliography *(Southern Illinois University, 1968). Dr. McCoy has assembled more than 8000 titles of monographs and articles from periodicals in the English language. Publications in other languages appear only rarely.*

For up-to-date censorship news the reader may wish to examine certain periodicals which are either completely dedicated to censorship or which comment with varying degrees of regularity on the activities of censors.

> *Newsletter on Intellectual Freedom* (American Library Association)
> *ALA Bulletin* (American Library Association)
> *Library Journal* (Bowker)
> *Publishers' Weekly* (Bowker)
> *FOI Digest* (University of Missouri)
> *Censorship Today* (Los Angeles)
> *Censorship* (London)

Blanshard, Paul. *American Freedom and Catholic Power.* 1960. *The Right to Read.* 1955.

Bowerman, George F. *Censorship and the Public Library.* 1931.

Boyer, Paul S. *Purity in Print.* 1968.

Bradbury, Ray. *Fahrenheit 451* (a novel). 1967.

Broun, Heywood and Margaret Leach. *Anthony Comstock: Roundsman of the Lord.* 1927.

Bury, John B. *A History of Freedom of Thought.* 1913.

Caughey, John W. *In Clear and Present Danger.* 1958.

Chafee, Zechariah, Jr. *Free Speech in the United States.* 1942. *Freedom of Speech.* 1920.

Cleaton, Irene and Allen Cleaton. *Books and Battles; American Literature, 1920–1930.* 1937.

Comstock, Anthony. *Traps for the Young.* 1883. Reprinted 1967.

Craig, Alec. *Above All Liberties.* 1942. *Suppressed Books.* 1963.

(Published the previous year in England with the title *The Banned Books of England and Other Countries.*)

Doob, Leonard W. *Public Opinion and Propaganda.* 2nd ed. 1966.

Douglas, William O. *The Right of the People.* 1958.

Downs, Robert B. ed. *The First Freedom* (an anthology). 1960.

Ernst, Morris L. *The First Freedom.* 1946.

Ernst, Morris L. and Alexander Lindey. *The Censor Marches On.* 1940.

Ernst, Morris L. and Alan U. Schwartz. *Censorship: The Search for the Obscene.* 1964.

Ernst, Morris L. and William Seagle. *To the Pure.* 1928.

Farrer, James A. *Books Condemned to be Burnt.* 1892.

Fellman, David. *The Censorship of Books.* 1957.

Fiske, Marjorie. *Book Selection and Censorship.* 1959.

Ford, John. *Criminal Obscenity, A Plea for its Suppression.* 1926.

Fowell, Frank and Frank Palmer. *Censorship in England.* 1913.

Franklin, Benjamin. *An Apology for Printers.* 1731.

Gardiner, Harold C. (S. J.). *Catholic Viewpoint on Censorship.* 1958.

Gellhorn, Walter. *Individual Freedom and Government Restraints.* 1956.

Gillett, Charles R. *Burned Books* 2v. 1932. Reprinted 1960.

Glasgow, Ellen. *Five Letters from Ellen Glasgow concerning Censorship* . . . 1962.

Hackett, Alice P. *Seventy Years of Best Sellers, 1895–1965.* 1967.

Haney, Robert W. *Comstockery in America.* 1960.

[Hewitt, Cecil R. ed.]. *The Trial of Lady Chatterley* . . . Edited by C. H. Rolph [pseud.]. 1961.

Hocking, William E. *Freedom of the Press.* 1947.

Hofstadter, Richard. *Anti-Intellectualism in American Life.* 1963.

Hudson, Edward G. *Freedom of Speech and Press in America.* 1963.

Hunnings, Neville M. *Film Censors and the Law.* 1967.

Hyde, H. Montgomery. *A History of Pornography.* 1964.

Index Librorum Prohibitorum. 1948.

Inglis, Brian. *The Freedom of the Press in Ireland.* 1954.

Inglis, Ruth A. *Freedom of the Movies.* 1947.

Jackson, Holbrook. *The Fear of Books.* 1932.

Johnson, Gerald W. *Peril and Promise: An Inquiry into Freedom of the Press.* 1958.

Kallen, Horace. *Indecency and the Seven Arts.* 1930.

Kilpatrick, James J. *The Smut Peddlers.* 1960.

Konvitz, Milton R. *First Amendment Freedoms.* 1963. *Fundamental Liberties of a Free People.* 1957.

Kronhausen, Eberhard and Phyllis Kronhausen. *Pornography and the Law.* 1959.

Kuh, Richard H. *Foolish Figleaves?* 1967.

Kyle-Keith, Richard. *The High Price of Pornography.* 1961.

Law, William. *Absolute Unlawfulness of the Stage-entertainment Fully Demonstrated.* 1726.

Lawrence, D. H. *Sex, Literature and Censorship.* ed. by Harry T. Moore. 1959.

Levy, Leonard W., ed. *Freedom of the Press from Zenger to Jefferson.* 1966.

Levy, Leonard W. *Legacy of Suppression: Freedom of Speech and Press in Early American History.* 1960.

Loth, David. *The Erotic in Literature.* 1961.

Marcus, Steven. *The Other Victorians.* 1966.

Marcuse, Ludwig. *Obscene; The History of an Indignation.* 1965.

McCormick, John and Mairi MacInnes, eds. *Versions of Censorship; An Anthology.* 1962.

McKeon, Richard P., R. K. Merton and Walter Gellhorn. *The Freedom to Read.* 1957.

Mill, John Stuart. *On Liberty.* 1859.

Milton, John. *Areopagitica.* 1644.

Minow, Newton N. *Equal Time; The Private Broadcaster and the Public Interest.* 1964.

Murphy, Terence J. *Censorship: Government and Obscenity.* 1963.

Nelson, Harold L., ed. *Freedom of The Press from Hamilton to the Warren Court.* 1967.

Patterson, Giles J. *Free Speech and a Free Press.* 1939.

Paul, James C. N. and Murray L. Schwartz. *Federal Censorship; Obscenity and the Mail.* 1961.

Putnam, George Haven. *Authors and their Public in Ancient Times.* 1923. *Books and their Makers During the Middle Ages* 2v. 1896. *The Censorship of the Church of Rome* 2v. 1907.

Rembar, Charles. *The End of Obscenity.* 1968.

Robinson, Victor, ed. *Encyclopaedia Sexualis.* 1936.

Schroeder, Theodore. *"Obscene" Literature and Constitutional Law.* 1911.

St. John-Stevas, Norman. *Obscenity and the Law.* 1956.

Taylor, G. Rattray. *Sex in History.* rev. ed. 1959.

Thayer, Frank. *Legal Control of the Press.* 4th ed. 1962.

Thompson, Elbert N. S. *The Controversy between the Puritans and the Stage.* 1903, repr. 1966.

Trumbull, Charles G. *Anthony Comstock, Fighter.* 1913.

Wickwar, William H. *The Struggle for the Freedom of the Press, 1819–1832*. 1928.

Widmer, Kingsley and Eleanor Widmer, eds. *Literary Censorship: Principles, Cases, Problems*. 1961.

Wiggins, James R. *Freedom or Secrecy*. 1956.

Index

Index

DATE DUE

Demco, Inc. 38-293